TRANSPORTED

50 VEHICLES THAT CHANGED THE WORLD

MATT RALPHS

nosy crow

RUI RICARDO

First published in 2022 by Nosy Crow Ltd
The Crow's Nest, 14 Baden Place,
Crosby Row, London, SE1 1YW, UK

Nosy Crow Eireann Ltd
44 Orchard Grove, Kenmare,
Co Kerry, V93 FY22, Ireland

www.nosycrow.com

ISBN 978 1 83994 217 4

Nosy Crow and associated logos are trademarks
and/or registered trademarks of Nosy Crow Ltd.

Text © Matt Ralphs 2022
Illustrations © Rui Ricardo 2022

The right of Matt Ralphs to be identified as the author and Rui Ricardo
to be identified as the illustrator of this work has been asserted.
All rights reserved.

Printed in China.
Papers used by Nosy Crow are made from wood
grown in sustainable forests.

1 3 5 7 9 8 6 4 2

CONTENTS

OUR JOURNEY BEGINS

Imagine a world without vehicles. No bikes, ships or rockets, no cars, trains or planes. Just you and your legs. How far could you walk in a day? Ten kilometres? Fifteen if you pushed yourself? And how much cargo could you carry on your back? Not much. You might be able to swim a river, even a lake if it wasn't too wide. But you certainly couldn't swim across an ocean or descend into its lightless depths. Or fly up to the sky, or even further into the endless expanse of space.

No. To do any of those things you'd need one of the 50 Vehicles That Changed the World.

The first vehicles were ships powered by the wind, and wagons and chariots pulled by oxen or horses. These pioneering contraptions allowed people in ancient times to travel far and wide, make connections with neighbouring countries, forge trading routes, and spread their culture and news. From that time thousands of years ago right up to the present day, people all over the world have stretched the boundaries of imagination, invention, science and technology to create the vast vehicle array examined on the following pages.

Some vehicles were designed for exploration and discovery. The Polynesian canoe allowed intrepid explorers to travel thousands of kilometres over the uncharted Pacific Ocean and make their homes on the islands they found there. The Norse used swift longships to navigate the seas and rivers of northern Europe – and even cross the Atlantic centuries before Christopher Columbus stepped aboard his sailing ship in 1492.

All vehicles transport us from one place to another, but some also keep us safe from hostile environments that would otherwise kill us. Submarines carry us deep under the ocean and provide protection from the crushing weight of the water and lack of oxygen; rockets and shuttles keep astronauts alive despite the freezing vacuum of space. Vehicles like these are not just a means of transport, they are life preservers, workspaces, homes.

Private vehicles such as the automobile, motorcycle and even the humble bike, have given ordinary people the freedom to travel wherever and whenever they want. Such easy and convenient mobility opens up opportunities to see new places, visit friends and family who live far away, and find jobs and recreational activities to enrich and improve our lives.

Vehicles can be lifesavers too. Fully equipped ambulances and fire engines driven by trained crews speed to emergencies with flashing lights and sirens; bush aeroplanes land deep in the wilderness to lend a hand when needed, and the versatile helicopter helps put out forest fires, and rescues people lost at sea or up mountains.

Some vehicles help feed us, like tractors that plough the fields and combine harvesters that reap the crops; others, like the truck and container ship, carry cargo all over the world; some wage war: the trireme, tank and battleship; and others entertain us, like super-fast Formula One cars.

All these vehicles and many more are waiting in this book to transport you on a fascinating journey from past to present, down highways, over rails, across continents, under oceans, above clouds, and even to faraway planets.

BON VOYAGE!

POLYNESIAN CANOE
OCEAN EXPLORERS

Several thousand years ago, ancient and adventurous seafarers set out from east Asia and travelled eastwards across the Pacific Ocean. Over the following centuries they discovered and settled on hundreds of islands, creating the group of nations and territories we now call Polynesia. Travel, trade and communication between these islands – some of which were thousands of kilometres apart – was made possible by the ancient Polynesians' incredible voyaging canoes and the navigators who steered them.

FACTS AND STATS

» **NAME:** Voyaging canoe
» **NUMBER OF HULLS:** 2
» **CREW:** 15–20
» **POWERED BY:** Sail and oars
» **AVERAGE SPEED:** 8–10 kph (approx.)
» **DIMENSIONS:** Length: 20 m (approx.); Average width: 6 m (approx.)

OCEAN EXPERTS

The Polynesians never saw the vast distances between their island homes as barriers, because their expert navigators knew the right pathways to take. They didn't need maps or mechanical pathfinding devices like compasses – all the information they required to find even the smallest and most remote island was provided by the natural world around them.

ONE THOUSAND ISLANDS

Polynesia (which means 'many islands') is a place unlike any other. Spread over a vast area of the Pacific Ocean, it's made up of more than 1,000 islands, some inhabited, some not; some big enough to have their own mountain ranges, others little more than sandy mounds covered in coconut trees. It forms a triangle, with Hawaii to the north, New Zealand to the west, and Rapa Nui (or Easter Island) to the east.

AN ANCIENT DESIGN PERFECTED

The ancient Polynesians built many different types of boat, but for long ocean journeys they used double-hulled canoes. Each hull was carefully hollowed out and shaped from a tree trunk, with sharp prows and sterns for slicing through the sea. Strong rope made from coconut fibres lashed everything together, and a simple shelter for the crew stood on the boards attached between the hulls. This wide design created a stable platform that was unlikely to capsize.

A MENTAL MAP

Navigators held in their mind a mental map of the stars. This allowed them, with a clear view of the night sky, to steer their canoe in the right direction by using the rising and setting points of the stars as markers, or 'waypoints'. For example, to head south they used a four-star constellation called the Southern Cross.

GUIDED BY NATURE

Navigators used other clues to get their bearings too: they looked out for fish that they knew swam near certain islands; or land-based plants or flowers floating on the surface; or followed birds back to shore – they could even see lagoons on faraway islands reflected on the underside of clouds.

WAYFARING BY WAVES

If it was cloudy and there were no stars to help, navigators used ocean swells that they knew always flowed in the same direction to find the right path to take. For example, if they knew a particular swell always travelled eastward, by sailing directly into the waves the boat would be heading west. Even in pitch-darkness a navigator could tell what direction their boat was going by feeling and listening to the way the waves hit the hull.

HOW THE POLYNESIAN CANOE CHANGED THE WORLD

The seafarers who set out on their voyaging canoes all those centuries ago had no knowledge of where they were going – the millions of square kilometres of ocean were a mystery. Yet, over many years of exploration, and with great courage and skill, they created Polynesia, turning a vast expanse of sea and 1,000 islands into their home, which still exists today.

BRONZE AGE WAGON
ANCIENT INVENTION

There was a time when there were no land vehicles. Even after prehistoric humans had started living together in settled communities, farmed the land and traded with each other, the only way to transport things across land was by hand or on the backs of animals like oxen or donkeys. And then, about 5,500 years ago, one of the most important inventions in history was made: the wheel, without which most of the land vehicles in this book would simply not exist. This Sumerian wagon is one of the very first land vehicles that we know about.

FIRST VEHICLES

It's hard to know exactly what the first Bronze Age wagons and carts looked like because there is very little detailed historical evidence left. We do know that the ancient Sumerian civilization (4500–1900 BC) from Mesopotamia built four-wheel wagons which might have looked like this one, because they included images of them on beautifully made mosaics. Pulled by four donkeys, steered with reins, solidly made from wood, and crewed by a driver and a warrior, it's possible they were used as transport to carry kings or generals around the battlefield, or as weapons to crash into enemy soldiers and scatter them.

FACTS AND STATS

» **WAGON TYPE:** War wagon

» **USED BY:** Ancient Sumerians, Mesopotamia

» **CREW:** 2

» **POWERED BY:** 4 donkeys or onagers (a type of horse)

» **TOP SPEED:** 25 kph (approx.)

» **DIMENSIONS:** Length (back of chariot to yoke): 3.4 m (approx.); Width: 2 m; Height: 1.3 m (approx.)

THE WORLD-CHANGING WHEEL

The oldest wheels ever found were dug up in Mesopotamia. They were made in around 3500 BC and were used horizontally as potters' wheels. The first wheels used for transport appeared a few centuries later and were made from solid wood (unspoked). To work on a vehicle, two wheels of the same size needed to be fitted, one at each end, to an axle. This provided balance and stability for the cart or wagon as it moved. Once discovered, the solid wheel spread quickly throughout Asia, the Middle East and Europe, and was later developed into the lighter, faster spoked version (see Ancient Chariot, page 10).

OLDEST WOODEN WHEEL

The oldest wooden wheel ever found was uncovered in the Ljubljana marshes in Central Europe, in a country we now call Slovenia. It is thought to be about 5,000 years old, which means it was made only slightly later than the first wheels being used in Mesopotamia. It was made from two pieces of ash wood held together with four cross braces, and measures 72 centimetres in diameter and is 5 centimetres thick. It was found with an intact oak wood axle, measuring 120 centimetres, and it is believed to have once been fixed to a handcart that would have been pushed by a person.

HOW THE BRONZE AGE WAGON CHANGED THE WORLD

Prehistoric wheeled vehicles like wagons and carts completely changed the way people lived their lives all those thousands of years ago. Whether hauled by animals like oxen, cows, onagers or donkeys, or pushed by human hands, they allowed heavy loads to be transported long distances in a way that had been completely impossible before. Wagons allowed farmers to carry their wares to market, builders to transport stone and lumber, and saved people from having to undertake exhausting journeys on foot. The wheeled wagon opened up the world and changed it forever.

ANCIENT CHARIOT

HIGH SPEED IN THE BRONZE AGE

For thousands of years, the fastest way for a human to move was to run as fast as they could. But after horses were tamed (around 3500 BC) and the wheel was invented (around 3000 BC), a brand-new way of travel was made possible. Hauled by two horses, the ancient two-wheeled chariot allowed people to journey at great speeds and over long distances for the very first time in history.

THE FIRST CHARIOTS

The oldest known two-wheeled chariots were found in burial mounds (graves) near the Ural mountains in what is now Russia; they were made by the Bronze Age Sintasha culture about 4,000 years ago. Expert metalworkers and tradespeople, the Sintasha sent their goods – and their chariots – to Asia and beyond. It was not long before many other cultures in India, China, Europe, the Middle East and North Africa learned about this remarkable vehicle design and began making their own versions.

FACTS AND STATS

» **PICTURED CHARIOT TYPE:** Ancient Egyptian war chariot
» **ERA OF DOMINANCE:** 2000–300 BC
» **CREW:** 2
» **POWERED BY:** 2 horses
» **TOP SPEED:** 60 kph (approx.)
» **DIMENSIONS:** Length (back of chariot to yoke): 3.4 m (approx.); Width: 2 m; Height: 1.3 m (approx.)

LIGHTWEIGHT AND LIGHTNING FAST

Whether being built for battles, hunts or races, a chariot's weight was of great importance: they had to be light so the horses could pull them at a gallop for long periods of time. They also had to be sturdy enough to take turns at high speed and over hard terrain. But while they were lightweight and fast, chariots were not very strong and could only travel safely over level and firm ground.

WARFARE ON WHEELS

Ancient Egyptian war chariots were designed for hit-and-run tactics, rushing close to enemy soldiers, shooting them with arrows, then retreating before the soldiers could fight back. A skilled archer could quickly move around the chariot, swapping sides to loose arrows in all directions while the driver concentrated on steering. Other ancient cultures, such as the Hittites, built stronger, slower, heavier chariots crewed by three men (driver, archer and a spear-and-shield man) that they used to ram into enemy formations. The largest chariot battle in history occurred in the Middle East in 1274 BC. The ancient Egyptians fought the Hittites at the Battle of Kadesh, and it's believed that each side had at least 2,000 war chariots.

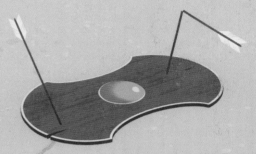

CHANGING CHARIOTS

Chariots were not just used in battle. Because they were expensive to build, they were driven by royalty and the rich to show off how wealthy and powerful they were. Chariots were also used for hunting: the driver chased the wild animal – often deer or big cats – while the passenger shot them with arrows. They were also used in races, most famously by the ancient Romans who built specially designed tracks in their cities, complete with thousands of seats for spectators.

HOW THE ANCIENT CHARIOT CHANGED THE WORLD

Historians are not sure which came first: people riding horses, or using horses to pull vehicles. What we do know is that humans created two-wheeled chariots in around 2000 BC, which allowed them to travel up to 60 kilometres per hour, much faster than a person can run. Chariots changed how battles were fought, allowed messages and news to spread quickly, and made hunting dangerous animals safer. Chariots were used all over Europe, the Middle East, North Africa and Asia, and they remained the fastest vehicle design in the world until the invention of the steam locomotive almost 4,000 years later.

TRIREME
SEABORNE BATTERING RAM

Triremes were the most advanced warships of the ancient world. Their narrow, streamlined hulls, powered by 170 rowers, allowed them to cut through water like knives and quickly change course in the heat of battle. Aside from the soldiers and archers prowling the deck, the trireme's main weapon was a devastating ram, designed to puncture enemy vessels and send them plunging to the bottom of the sea.

FACTS AND STATS

» **VESSEL TYPE:** Warship
» **USED MAINLY BY:** Ancient Greeks, Romans, Persians and Phoenicians
» **ERA OF DOMINANCE:** 7th–4th centuries BC
» **CREW:** 200
» **POWERED BY:** 2 sails and 170 oars
» **AVERAGE SPEED:** 11 kph
» **RANGE:** 80–100 km per day
» **WEAPONS:** Bronze ram
» **DIMENSIONS:** Length: 36 m; Width (or 'Beam'): 5 m

BUILDING THE HULL

Building a trireme was expensive and took thousands of hours of skilled labour. The hull was made using the light, strong timber from fir, pine and cedar trees. The keel at the bottom was made from stronger oak, which would not be damaged when the ship was hauled onto rocky beaches at the end of a day's voyage. Triremes were often brightly decorated, with fearsome eyes painted above the ram.

ROWERS

Working below deck were 170 highly trained rowers. Each had their own oar and a cushion to sit on. Rowers sat in three levels inside the ship. Most had no view of the sea and relied on their superintendent to give them orders. Rowers on the bottom level were often soaked by water splashing in through the oar holes.

CAPTAIN

A trireme, like this one from the Greek city of Athens, was captained by a 'trierarch'. Trierarchs were usually wealthy citizens, and it was their duty to pay the crew and keep the ship battle-ready.

DECK CREW

The deck crew sailed, steered and maintained the ship. The helmsman (*kybernetes*) was in charge and steered the vessel. The bow lookout (*proreus*) kept watch for landmarks, shallow waters and other ships; the boatswain (*keleustes*) looked after the hull; the quartermaster (*pentekontarchos*) organised equipment and provisions; the shipwright (*naupegos*) carried out repairs; a piper (*auletes*) played to give the oarsmen a rhythm to row to; two superintendents (*toicharchoi*) were in charge of the rowers, and 10 sailors handled the masts and sails.

HOW THE TRIREME CHANGED THE WORLD

Many wars were fought between the ancient Greeks and Persians – there were huge invasions, desperate defences, regions captured and then freed after massive battles on land and at sea. At the centre of all this turmoil were the trireme war fleets, which took part in naval actions (such as the Battle of Artemisium) that helped shape the countries and cultures of southern Europe, the Middle East and North Africa.

SOLDIERS AT SEA

One way that triremes were used in battle was to get close enough to an enemy ship to allow the soldiers to leap on board and attack the crew. To carry out this dangerous duty, ancient Greek triremes had 10–20 *hoplites* (soldiers armed with shields, swords and spears) and four archers to shoot arrows. These onboard soldiers were vital for defending the oarsmen if their own ship was boarded.

SHORT TRIPS ONLY

Triremes were not designed for long voyages and rarely travelled far from land. They didn't carry much food and their hulls became waterlogged if they stayed at sea for too long, so they had to be dragged onto beaches at night. However, triremes were so light that the crew could haul them out of the water with ropes.

RAM

Triremes were not just ships – they were weapons. A trireme could close in on an enemy vessel at top speed, crash into their hull, and reverse away as fast as possible. A successful ramming attack shattered oars, terrified crew, and caused flooding through the hull.

VIKING LONGSHIP
FAST AND FRIGHTENING

The Vikings' homeland was forested and mountainous, which meant it was easier to travel over water than land. They became expert boatbuilders who designed the most advanced and successful vessel of their era – the longship. There was nothing more terrifying than seeing one of these boats slice towards you through the waves, oars dipping, blood-red sail fat with wind, and carrying a crew of axe-wielding warriors.

THE VIKINGS

Vikings are also called Norsemen ('men of the north'). They came from the area of northern Europe that we now call Scandinavia, which is comprised of Sweden, Denmark and Norway. From around 790 to 1066 AD, the Vikings ruled the waves, striking out from their chilly homelands to kill, pillage and capture people as slaves. But Vikings were not just raiders – they were also brave explorers, and skilled craftworkers and traders.

FIGUREHEAD

Vikings loved to carve fearsome figureheads for their ships, often in the shape of dragons; it's possible they believed these would scare away evil spirits.

SAIL POWER

On long journeys, Vikings unfurled the sail and let the wind do the work. Often dyed bright colours, these large, square sails were made from wool, and could be raised or lowered in a matter of minutes.

FACTS AND STATS

» **ALSO CALLED:** Dragonship
» **CREW:** 35–70
» **POWERED BY:** Sails and 20–30 oars
» **TOP SPEED:** 25 kph
» **DIMENSIONS:** Length: 14–23 m; Width (or 'Beam'): 2.5–4 m; Height: 16–20 m

CONSTRUCTING THE HULL

The keel of a longship was carved from oak, which is strong and takes ages to rot away. Overlapping planks were then fastened lengthwise to each other with iron nails, and gaps between the planks were stuffed with animal hair and wool to keep out water. Horizontal timbers were braced across the bottom to add strength, then the wooden deck was placed on top. Finally, the finished hull was waterproofed with tar.

A FAST ATTACK VEHICLE

The Vikings designed their longships to be swift through the water, strong and flexible enough to survive long voyages in heavy seas, capable of sailing up rivers, and light enough for the crew to carry them over land. This allowed them to go pretty much anywhere, which meant that no one was safe from Viking attack.

HOW THE VIKING LONGSHIP CHANGED THE WORLD

For almost 300 years, the strong, adventurous Vikings reigned supreme over the seas of northern Europe – no other nation could match their ships or sailing skills. Their incredible multi-purpose longships allowed them to raid, trade and eventually settle in Britain, northern France, Russia, the Mediterranean and beyond – even as far as North America.

LIFE ON BOARD

The men crewing longships had to be many things: sailors, warriors, explorers, traders, even settlers in new lands. They had to be extra tough on long ocean voyages, where they would be exposed to cold lashing rain and stormy seas, and have to put up with stale food, rancid water and endless hours of rowing.

FORWARDS AND BACKWARDS

The bow and stern were the same shape, which meant the ship could travel as quickly backwards as it could forwards (when powered by oars).

OAR POWER

If there was no wind, or it was blowing in the wrong direction, the longship was powered by oars, which were fitted through holes cut into the hull. Rowing was hard work, but it kept the Vikings strong. Rowers sat on chests called 'thwarts', which contained their belongings. Weapons and food were stored under loose deck-boards.

BALLAST

Large stones were laid out over the keel to help keep the boat stable.

RUDDER

The helmsman used a rudder to steer the ship.

NARROWBOAT
CARGO ON THE CANALS

There's always something to see along Britain's 5,000 kilometres of preserved canal network: red-brick bridges, leaking lock gates, and if you're lucky, the magical blue streak of a speeding kingfisher. But these canals were built to create money, not beauty. They were the main roads of their day, and the cargo-laden narrowboats that travelled them for two centuries helped turn Britain into a powerful and wealthy nation.

FACTS AND STATS

» **BOAT TYPE:** Narrowboat or canalboat (not barge)

» **SERVICE LIFE:** Late 1700s to present day

» **CREW:** 2 (min.)

» **POWERED BY:** Horse, steam or diesel

» **CARGO CAPACITY:** 35 tonnes (approx.)

» **AVERAGE SPEED:** 5–6 kph (approx.)

» **DIMENSIONS:** Maximum length: 23 m; Width (or 'Beam'): 2 m

CANAL MANIA

Cargo had been transported in boats over Britain's natural waterways for centuries because it was far easier and quicker than doing so by road. However, the boats could only go where the rivers went. Wealthy factory and business owners solved this problem in the late 1700s when they decided to build their own waterways. This was a massive and expensive undertaking, but these artificial rivers – called 'canals' – quickly became the fastest, most reliable and money-making way to transport cargo.

A HOME ON THE WATER

A narrowboat crew or family lived together in a brightly decorated cabin. Inside was a stove to cook on and keep warm by in the winter, cupboards for food and kitchenware, and beds. Water was kept in buckets, and there was no toilet or sink. It could be cosy for one or two people, but for a family it was cramped and uncomfortable.

FROM PORT TO FACTORY AND BACK AGAIN

Teams of workers called 'navvies' (navigational engineers) created a massive network of canals across Britain, linking the major cities (such as Manchester, Birmingham, Leeds and Liverpool) to coastal ports. This allowed ships to offload goods bought from other countries, like cotton or tea, onto narrowboats which delivered them to inland factories. The narrowboats were then loaded up with finished products which they carried back to the ships to be sold overseas.

ENGINE POWER

The early 1900s saw the introduction of narrowboats powered by coal-fired steam engines. Diesel engines followed, and they were more powerful, reliable and easier to operate.

CARGO CAPACITY

Most of the space in a narrowboat was used for cargo, whether it was loose coal or gravel, bricks, roof tiles, barrels of beer, bales of cotton, rolls of linen, boxes of biscuits or bottles of lemonade.

HORSEPOWER

Early narrowboats were towed by horses, which is why pathways alongside canals are called 'towpaths'. Attached by a rope, the horse plodded along led by a member of the crew. Narrowboats were often crewed by families who lived in a shared cabin. Everyone helped to steer the boat, lead the horse, work the locks and load cargo. It was a tough life – families worked long into the night and in all weathers, because the more cargo they delivered, the more money they earned.

HOW THE NARROWBOAT CHANGED THE WORLD

Narrowboats helped fuel the Industrial Revolution, a time when Britain became wealthy by producing and selling goods all over the world. They hauled the coal needed to fire up the ironworks, the raw materials to supply the factories, and they carried the goods produced to markets, warehouses and ports. The horse and cart could not hope to compete with the speed and ease with which the narrowboats cruised through the water, hauling tonnes of cargo for kilometres without rest.

HOT-AIR BALLOON

UP, UP AND AWAY!

In 1783, on a chilly but bright winter's day in France, a truly historic event took place. In front of a huge crowd, two men – a chemistry teacher and a soldier – were lifted from the ground by a beautiful blue hot-air balloon and drifted away over Paris. They were the first humans ever to fly, and we can only imagine how they felt as they gazed down like birds onto the world far below.

THE MONTGOLFIER BROTHERS

The first hot-air balloons were invented by French brothers Joseph-Michel and Jacques-Étienne Montgolfier. Joseph's first experiment with hot air involved him lighting a fire beneath a light wooden box and watching in astonishment as it shot up and hit the ceiling. From then the brothers continued to experiment, eventually replacing wooden boxes with large, airtight sackcloth bags covered on the inside with layers of paper. Their goal was to create a lighter-than-air vehicle that could lift a person.

FACTS AND STATS

» BALLOON NAME: *Aerostatic Globe*
» DESIGNED BY: Joseph-Michel and Jacques-Étienne Montgolfier
» FIRST MANNED AND TETHERED LAUNCH: 15 October 1783
» FIRST MANNED AND UNTETHERED LAUNCH: 21 November 1783
» ALTITUDE REACHED: 910 m
» DISTANCE TRAVELLED: 9 km
» CREW: 2
» AVERAGE SPEED: 8–16 kph
» DIMENSIONS: Height: 23 m; Width: 15 m; Weight: 780 kg; Lifting capacity: 800 kg; Gas volume: 2,000 m²

PIONEER BALLOONISTS

No one knew what flying high in the air would do to the human body. King Louis XVI, the king of France, suggested sending up prisoners to see what would happen, but the Montgolfier brothers were not keen on that idea. Instead, they used a sheep, a duck and a rooster. In September 1783, a balloon was released with the animals dangling below in a wicker basket. They drifted for about three kilometres before touching down, startled but unharmed, in some woods. It was now time to send people into the sky.

GETTING ALOFT

The *Aerostatic Globe* needed to be filled with hot air, which is lighter than cool air and so made the balloon float. The opening at the bottom of the envelope was placed above a fire until it was ready to fly. Two poles kept it anchored to the ground. Then, when the ropes were untied, the *Aerostatic Globe* could float away. Modern hot-air balloons work in a similar way: hot air made by burning liquidised gas fills a nylon or polyester envelope, and passengers travel in a gondola hanging below.

HOW THE HOT-AIR BALLOON CHANGED THE WORLD

Hot-air balloons were the very first vehicle that allowed people to fly, so it's no wonder that they caught the imagination of the world. It was not long before armies made use of them for scouting enemy positions during battles. The fact hot-air balloons couldn't be steered and flew whichever way the wind took them meant they didn't end up being used as a reliable form of transportation, but it's likely their existence inspired later inventors to come up with flying vehicles of their own.

FRIENDS IN HIGH PLACES

The Montgolfiers' successful experiments with lighter-than-air flight soon caught the interest of the Royal Academy of Science and Louis XVI. Before long the whole country was fascinated by hot-air balloons. The Montgolfiers' public demonstrations were often held in front of the royal family, nobility and important people from all over the world.

WOODEN BATTLESHIP
MASTS, SAILS AND BROADSIDES

Built to shatter enemy vessels with devastating volleys of cannon fire, the *Santísima Trinidad* was the first four-decked battleship in the world and was armed with more guns than any other vessel at the time. However, her huge bulk made her hard to steer and easy to hit. Her final fight was against the British Royal Navy at the famous Battle of Trafalgar in 1805 where she was damaged, captured and finally sunk in a storm a few days later – a sad fate for such an awesome ship.

SAILS, RIGGING AND RATLINES

The *Santísima Trinidad* was powered by wind. Each sail had to be lowered (to slow the ship down) or raised (to speed it up) by hand. Teams of sailors climbed up rope ladders (called 'ratlines') and then shimmied along the horizontal beams ('yards' or 'spars') using 'footropes'. It took a long time for a sailor to fully 'learn the ropes', and it was a dangerous job: they were high up, had no safety equipment, and falling meant serious injury or death.

FACTS AND STATS

- » **VESSEL NAME:** *Santísima Trinidad*
- » **VESSEL TYPE:** First rate ship of the line
- » **BUILT IN:** Havana, Cuba
- » **OWNED BY:** Spanish Navy
- » **SERVICE LIFE:** 1769–1805
- » **CREW:** 1,200 (approx.)
- » **TOP SPEED:** 18 kph (approx.)
- » **MAXIMUM ARMAMENT:** 140 guns
- » **DIMENSIONS:** Length: 61.3 m; Width (or 'Beam'): 16.2 m; Weight: 4,950 tonnes

WOODEN WALLS

It took hundreds of skilled workers and lots of time and materials to build a wooden battleship. Thousands of carefully chosen trees were cut down and allowed to 'season' (dry out) for over a decade before being used to build keels, hulls, decks, railings, bulkheads, masts and spars. Some ships had their bottoms covered in copper sheets to prevent barnacles and seaweed build-up from slowing them down, and rot and woodworm from weakening the hull.

HOW THE WOODEN BATTLESHIP CHANGED THE WORLD

Wooden battleships like the *Santísima Trinidad* were important to Great Britain, France and Spain, the most powerful European nations of the 18th and 19th centuries. From the Atlantic to the Pacific to the Indian Oceans, these huge, floating gun platforms were used to patrol the seas and protect valuable cargo vessels. All this, and the naval battles in which they fought, such as the Battle of Trafalgar, helped shape the world as we know it today.

A SAILOR'S LIFE

Life for sailors was hard. They'd spend hours each day scrubbing the decks, scurrying up ratlines, mending sails and practising firing the cannons. Anyone who broke the rules was severely punished. However, sailors were guaranteed three hot meals a day. They ate salted fish, beef and pork, cheese, bread, biscuits, oatmeal and soups, and drank watered-down beer or wine. Most sailors slept in hammocks strung up between the cannons on the gun decks.

BATTLE STATIONS

In battle, captains were not usually trying to sink enemy ships (it was far better to capture these valuable vehicles intact). Instead, they aimed to cause as much damage and disorder as possible by firing through the hull. Another tactic was to disable enemy ships by shooting 'chain shot' – a length of chain with a weight at each end – which sliced through and destroyed masts, sails, ratlines and spars.

GUNSHIP

Santísima Trinidad began her service as a three-decker with 112 guns – until the Spanish Navy decided that this simply wasn't deadly enough. So they added a fourth gun deck and another 28 guns to make her the most heavily armed vessel afloat. Cannons were usually fired one after the other in a rapid ripple effect, and only occasionally all at once (a 'broadside') because of the huge strain that put on the ship's timbers.

STAGECOACH

HORSEPOWER

Travellers taking a long journey in the 1800s might have gone by stagecoach. Pulled by teams of strong, well-bred horses, these lightweight, suspension-equipped vehicles clattered along roads much faster than heavier farm carts. However, every wheel rut, pothole or sharp corner would jolt the stagecoach, as well as the tightly packed passengers inside and clinging onto the roof.

THE STAGECOACH

Stagecoaches were large wooden carriages with four wheels. The driver, or 'coachman', sat at the front (sometimes with a guard) controlling his horse team with reins and a whip; coachmen usually drove about 80 kilometres in a long day before a new one took over. There was room inside for up to six passengers. Tickets for a seat on the roof cost half as much, but the passengers had to put up with whatever the weather threw at them.

FACTS AND STATS

» **CREW:** 1 driver (and sometimes a guard)
» **POWERED BY:** Teams of 4 or 6 horses
» **TOP SPEED:** 9–18 kph
» **PASSENGERS:** 12
» **DIMENSIONS:** Length: 4.1 m; Width: 1.8 m; Height: 2.7 m

DANGER ON THE ROAD

Travelling by stagecoach could be dangerous and accidents were common. If the horses panicked and bolted, or a wheel broke or slid into a ditch, stagecoaches were likely to overturn, especially if they were top-heavy with baggage and passengers loaded onto the roof. Accidents like this could easily cause injury and even death. There was also the chance of being held up by highwaymen – armed robbers who'd lay in wait on the roadside then leap out brandishing pistols and threats. Stagecoaches sometimes employed guards to see them off.

A BUMPY RIDE

Although stagecoaches were one of the fastest ways to travel, journeys could still take several days. Passengers inside were crammed together, sometimes for hours at a time, enduring coach-sickness caused by every judder and jolt. Travelling on the roof was even worse due to the ever-present danger of tumbling off.

COACHING INNS

Journeys were split up into stages (this is where the term 'stagecoach' comes from) because the horse teams needed to rest every 15 kilometres or so. Each stage had a coaching inn (a public house and hotel with stables attached) where the horses were replaced and the passengers had the chance to enjoy a drink, have a bite to eat and go to the toilet before continuing on their way.

HOW THE STAGECOACH CHANGED THE WORLD

The stagecoach and the improved roads they sped down allowed passengers, letters and parcels to be transported more quickly and safely than ever before, even in the depths of winter: a journey of weeks now took days; a journey of days now took hours. Although tickets were not cheap, stagecoach companies offered the chance for ordinary people to travel further afield than they ever would have been able to before.

THE HORSES

Stagecoach horses were chosen for their speed, strength and stamina. They were usually owned by coaching-inn managers, who hired them out to the stagecoach companies. In the morning, a horse team pulled a coach to the next inn along the road. Then they were taken off that stagecoach, rested and fed. In the afternoon, they were hitched to another stagecoach going back to the first coaching inn, due to arrive in the evening – a round trip of around 30 kilometres.

THE ROAD TO SUCCESS

Up until the late 1700s, most roads throughout Britain and Europe were little more than rutted dirt tracks. Travelling on foot, horse or wagon was a slow, painstaking trudge, especially in winter when the surface was either rock-hard and icy, or waterlogged and muddy. Eventually roads were straightened, levelled out and weatherproofed, allowing stagecoaches to travel faster and reducing the number of accidents.

STEAM LOCOMOTIVE
THE RADICAL ROCKET

In the early 1800s, a strange addition appeared on the landscape of northern England: two sets of gleaming steel rails cutting a curved path through the fields. Onlookers watched as a white smudge of smoke and a faint chuffing sound emerged from the trees, and then a bright yellow machine appeared, billowing steam and clanking up the rails faster than a galloping horse. This was the steam locomotive *Rocket*, and a transport revolution set to change the world followed close behind.

STEAMING ALONG

Engineer Robert Stephenson knew how a steam locomotive worked when he sat at his desk to design *Rocket*. Coal (or 'coke') is burned in the loco's 'firebox', which boils water in the boiler. Steam created by the boiling water is directed through pipes into pistons to make them move. Each piston has a 'driving rod' connected to a 'driving wheel'. As the pistons pump up and down, the driving rods turn the driving wheels and the loco begins to move. Smoke from the fire shoots up the chimney, creating a chuffing sound.

FACTS AND STATS

» **ENGINE NAME:** *Rocket*
» **DESIGNED BY:** Robert Stephenson
» **BUILT BY:** Robert Stephenson and Company, Newcastle-Upon-Tyne, UK
» **CONSTRUCTION DATE:** 1829
» **USED ON:** Liverpool & Manchester Railway
» **CREW:** 2 (engineer and stoker)
» **FUEL TYPE:** Coke (a type of refined coal)
» **TOP SPEED:** 48 kph
» **DIMENSIONS:** Length: 4.2 m (including tender); Width: 1.85 m; Height: 4.9 m (to chimney top); Weight: 4.3 tonnes

THE RAINHILL TRIALS

By 1829, the new Liverpool & Manchester Railway needed to decide what steam locomotive to use. So, they invited engineers to demonstrate their inventions, with the winner receiving £500 (about £50,000 today). Five locos took part, including one powered by a horse. In front of thousands of onlookers, these hissing and smoke-spewing contraptions took turns to pull loaded wagons until, one by one, they broke down. Only Stephenson's *Rocket* successfully completed the trials.

MULTI-TUBULAR BOILER

Most early locos had one or two copper fire-tubes running from the firebox into the water-filled boiler; when the fire-tubes got hot, they boiled the water. However, Stephenson decided to increase this number to 25 fire-tubes, expanding the hot surface area inside the boiler and making heating the water faster and more fuel-efficient.

HOW THE STEAM LOCOMOTIVE CHANGED THE WORLD

Using Stephenson's incredible *Rocket*, the Liverpool & Manchester Railway was an immediate success, and soon many other railways running steam locomotives were completed to carry passengers and freight. Within 20 years, 10,000 kilometres of railways had been built in Britain. Steam locomotives were much faster than narrowboats and, as designs improved, became extremely reliable and capable of hauling huge loads over long distances. For the next 150 years they were used in their tens of thousands all over the world.

ANGLED PISTONS

Up until 1829, most steam locomotives had vertical driving pistons, which caused the loco to sway from side to side. Stephenson set *Rocket*'s pistons at an angle close to horizontal, which made for a much smoother and stabler ride.

AN OVERLOOKED PIONEER

The very first steam locomotive to run on rails was designed by a Cornish engineer called Richard Trevithick. He used a stationary steam engine built to drive an industrial hammer (also his design) at the Penydarren Ironworks in Wales and converted it to run on wheels. In February 1804 his great invention clattered and puffed for 16 kilometres, hauling an impressive load of 10 tonnes of iron and 70 men. Stephenson combined the most successful elements from this and other earlier steam loco designs into his *Rocket*, and for the next 150 years nearly every steam locomotive copied his template.

TWO DRIVING WHEELS

Stephenson only used one pair of driving wheels (wheels moved by the pistons and driving rods) for *Rocket*, rather than the more usual four; the pair at the back were unpowered. This made the vehicle's design simpler and ensured that mechanical failures were less likely.

ROCKET

SUBMARINE
BENEATH THE WAVES

Oceans cover 70 per cent of our planet, and much of what goes on beneath the waves is still a mystery to us. It's a dangerous place to explore: there's no oxygen to breathe, and with every descending metre the temperature lowers, pressure increases to deadly levels, and sunlight fades to gloom . . . then complete darkness. Yet humans have been compelled to explore this alien environment and study the strange and wonderful creatures that live there for centuries – leading to many pioneering submarines, such as the *Ictineo II*.

FACTS AND STATS

» **SUBMARINE NAME:** *Ictineo II*
» **DESIGNED BY:** Narcís Monturiol
» **SERVICE LIFE:** May 1865– December 1867
» **CREW:** Captain plus 4 crew
» **POWERED BY:** Propeller driven by an air-independent steam engine
» **AVERAGE SPEED:** 8 kph
» **DEEPEST DIVE:** 30 m
» **NUMBER OF HULLS:** 2 (inner and outer)
» **DIMENSIONS:** Length: 14 m; Width: 2 m; Height: 3 m

SUBMERGIBLE STEAM ENGINE

In 1864, a Spanish engineer called Narcís Monturiol launched the *Ictineo II*, a submarine he'd designed and built, and the first to be powered by an engine. It used a steam engine to turn the propeller, but because fires can't be used inside a submarine (they use up all the oxygen), Monturiol devised an ingenious method of heating the steam engine's water by using a chemical reaction. As an added bonus, this chemical reaction produced oxygen for the crew to breathe as they went about their underwater work.

A LEAKY, HAND-POWERED PIONEER

One of the very first submersible vehicles was called *Turtle*. Built in North America in 1775, it was pear-shaped, just big enough for one person to sit in, and built from oak planks and iron. It was designed to sneak up on enemy ships and plant explosives onto their hulls. *Turtle* was equipped with a hand-operated rudder and propellers, a depth gauge, compass, and a hatch with viewing windows. The most nerve-wracking part of *Turtle*'s design was that there were no ballast tanks, so the water that was let inside to submerge the sub swirled around the pilot's legs. *Turtle* was slow, awkward to operate and failed to sink any ships, but worked as a submarine.

MODERN SUBMARINES

It took decades of experimentation before submarines became safe and reliable. The most produced submarine in history was the German-built diesel-electric Type VII U-boat, with 703 manufactured between 1936 and 1945. They could stay at sea for months and dive up to 230 metres. In 1954, USS *Nautilus*, the first nuclear-powered sub, was launched. *Nautilus* didn't need to refuel, could travel up to 43 kilometres per hour and remain underwater for months. In 1958 she did something no submarine had ever done before and travelled 1,600 kilometres under the ice to reach the North Pole.

TWO HULLS, EIGHT TANKS

To submerge the *Ictineo II*, eight ballast tanks were filled with water; to surface, they were pumped full of air. It was steered by a crew member who sat in the conning tower, looking out through glass windows. Like most modern submarines, *Ictineo II* had two hulls. The inner 'pressure' hull was watertight and kept the crew safe and dry. The outer hull was streamlined and smooth, allowing it to glide through the water. Of all the many early experimental submarines, *Ictineo II* was one of the safest and most successful.

HOW THE SUBMARINE CHANGED THE WORLD

Whether designed for warfare or research, submarines have changed a lot since *Turtle* first bobbed about beneath the water: they can reach great depths, travel for thousands of kilometres without surfacing, and keep their crews safe from the dangers of underwater travel. With every dive they make, we learn more about the mysteries kept at the bottom of our endless oceans.

STEAMSHIP
BOILERS, PADDLES AND PROPELLERS

During the 19th century, the Mississippi river was home to hundreds of paddle steamers. As white and ornate as wedding cakes, they were driven through the wide river waters, steam engines belching smoke and flames. On deck, passengers watched towns and countryside glide by; inside, they ate lavish meals, played games and socialised in opulent halls lit by crystal chandeliers and stained-glass skylights. Packed with cargo (including, sometimes, enslaved people), holidaymakers and American adventurers, these grand ships churned water into froth for 100 years.

FACTS AND STATS

» **VESSEL NAME:** *Natchez VI*
» **BUILT IN:** Cincinnati, USA
» **SERVICE LIFE:** 1869–1879
» **NUMBER OF VOYAGES:** 401
» **CREW:** 50 (approx.)
» **CARGO CAPACITY:** 5,500 bales of cotton
» **AVERAGE SPEED:** 12–15 kph
» **PADDLE SIZE:** Diameter: 13 m; Width: 3.3 m
» **DIMENSIONS:** Length: 92 m; Width: 14 m; Height: 10 m

ROLLING ON A RIVER

In the 1810s, there were only 20 paddle steamers like the *Natchez* churning up and down the 6,000-kilometre-long Mississippi river – by the 1830s, there were over 1,200. These vessels were perfect for carrying passengers and merchants, as well as cargoes of cotton, rice, timber and tobacco. Their shallow drafts meant they were less likely to be grounded on sandbanks, and the huge chimney stacks were lowered to go under bridges.

FROM SAIL TO STEAM

The first boats powered by steam engines and paddles appeared in the late 1700s, but most were underpowered, often broke down and were totally unsuitable for long voyages. However, engineers saw the huge potential of steam-powered vessels and continued to create lighter and more powerful engines. By the mid-1800s, paddle-driven steamboats were being used worldwide to carry passengers and cargo up rivers, and across lakes and channels.

HOW THE STEAMSHIP CHANGED THE WORLD

Whether tramping up winding rivers on churning paddles or cutting across oceans using whirling screws, steamships changed the world forever – and for the worse for the enslaved people they sometimes transported. Unlike sailing ships, they didn't depend on the unreliable wind – as long as they had enough fuel and a working engine, steamships could travel wherever they wanted. This allowed the creation of brand-new trade routes, and gave millions of people the opportunity to travel more swiftly and safely all over the world.

DANGEROUS LUXURY

Ornately decorated and brightly lit, Mississippi paddle steamers were built like floating palaces to entice fun-loving people on board. However, the steam-engine boilers were often badly made and pushed beyond their safety limits by speed-hungry captains. About 7,000 people were killed in boiler explosions between 1811 and 1853.

FROM STEAMBOATS TO STEAMSHIPS

Seeing the success of the steamboat, merchants and shipping companies knew a lot of money could be made if they could build a reliable ocean-going steamship. The first paddle-driven steamship specially designed to cross the Atlantic was the SS *Great Western*, designed by the engineering genius Isambard Kingdom Brunel and launched in 1837. The first paddle-driven iron steamship, the SS *Great Eastern* (another Brunel design), launched in 1858. She was a true giant, remaining the longest ship (at 211 metres) for the next 40 years, and capable of carrying 4,000 passengers from Britain to Australia without stopping to refuel.

SLAVE LABOUR ON PADDLE STEAMERS

Although the invention of the steamship was celebrated the world over, it was also used for some terrible things. Up until 1865, slavery was legal in 11 southern states in North America, and some paddle steamer companies owned Black enslaved people or were paid to transport them around the country. Enslaved people working on paddle steamers were usually given the hardest tasks, such as stoking fuel into the boilers and loading and unloading cargo. Enslaved men, women and children being transported were chained together, underfed and exposed to all weathers. All enslaved people were subjected to terrible violence and abuse. Some did manage to escape to the 'free' north of America by stowing away on paddle steamers.

EARLY BICYCLE

REVOLUTIONARY WHEELS

Only the most adventurous of Victorian travellers dared clamber into the saddle of one of these strange contraptions. It's one of many early bicycle designs, but this model – called the penny-farthing – was incredibly popular during the 1870s and 1880s. Penny-farthings were difficult to master and it was painful (and easy) to fall off, but they gave people freedom to travel far and wide, and with much less effort than by walking.

GETTING ON AND OFF

Mounting a penny-farthing was tricky and required quite a bit of skill. The rider put one foot on a bar over the back wheel, while gripping the handlebars. They then set the bike moving, boosted themselves up, settled into the seat and finally put both feet onto the pedals. During all this, they also had to steer and keep their balance. To get off, this process was repeated in reverse.

ACCIDENT PRONE

Although the large front wheel created quite a fast and comfortable ride, its height made the bike hard to control. Accidents were common as any sudden stop (if the wheel got stuck in a pothole, for example) could cause the rider to 'take a header' – hurtle over the handlebars and fall head first to the ground.

FRAME, FORKS AND HANDLEBARS

The frame was made from a piece of hollow steel tubing, which split into a fork at the bottom for the small wheel (called the 'farthing', named after the small British coin). The longer fork for the large front wheel (called the 'penny', named after the large British coin) was attached to the top of the frame and could be moved left and right with the handlebars to steer. A simple brake slowed the bike down.

SADDLE

A leather saddle was attached to the frame; a spring made it more comfortable to sit on.

FACTS AND STATS

» **BICYCLE NAME:** Penny-farthing (also called 'high wheelers' and 'ordinary bicycles')

» **DESIGN TYPE:** Direct drive bicycle

» **DESIGNED BY:** Eugène Meyer

» **DESIGNED IN:** 1869

» **POWERED BY:** Legs driving pedals

» **AVERAGE SPEED:** 8-12 kph

» **DIMENSIONS:** Front wheel diameter: 1.5 m

TYRES

Penny-farthings had solid rubber tyres around a spoked wheel, which made the ride smoother over uneven ground like paving stones and cobbles.

THE PENNY

The most unique part of the penny-farthing is the huge front wheel. When the rider pushed on the pedals, they turned this wheel without the use of a chain (this is called a 'direct drive' system). The front wheel's large size meant that one pedal turn was converted into a lot of travelled distance, making them faster than other bicycles of the time.

HOW THE EARLY BICYCLE CHANGED THE WORLD

For centuries, the only way a person could quickly cover long distances was by horse – the problem was horses were expensive and ordinary people couldn't afford them. However, the invention of the penny-farthing, and eventually the mass-produced bicycle, changed everything. This simple machine gave everybody the ability to travel many kilometres, at speed, using their own leg-power. A cycling craze swept the world, and it's still going strong today.

EVOLUTION OF THE BICYCLE

A German inventor called Karl Drais invented the first two-wheeled, steerable, human-powered vehicle in the early 1800s. Many more designs followed but they were usually too expensive for ordinary people. Everything changed with Eugene Meyer's penny-farthing, and his invention became immensely popular with adventurous travellers. Soon afterwards the 'safety bicycle' was developed – so-called because it was less dangerous to ride than the penny-farthing. With its triangular frame and chain connecting the pedals to the back wheel, it's just like the bikes we ride today, over 100 years later.

TEA CLIPPER
MAJESTIC MERCHANTMEN

The famous tea clipper *Cutty Sark* was designed with one thing in mind: speed. That's because in the mid-1800s, rival vessels competed in the race to carry tea from China to Great Britain as fast as possible. Straining every line and with acres of sail catching the wind, these beautiful ships tore down the South China Sea, across the Indian and Atlantic Oceans, then up the English Channel and the Thames to offload their precious cargo in record-breaking times.

CLIPPING THE WAVES

In the 1800s, tea was an expensive luxury in Great Britain. Every tea merchant in London wanted their share of the harvest from faraway China to reach the docks before their rivals' so they could be the first to sell it, and because customers believed that fresh leaves tasted better. To serve this need for speed, naval engineers designed a new type of vessel – the 'clipper'. Although they couldn't carry as much in their holds, these ships made the journey three times faster than the heavy old East Indiamen cargo vessels that they replaced. *Cutty Sark* was one of the swiftest clippers, and held the speed record from Australia to England – only 73 days – for 10 years.

FACTS AND STATS

» **VESSEL NAME:** *Cutty Sark*
» **DESIGNED BY:** Hercules Linton
» **BUILT BY:** Scott & Linton, Scotland
» **OPERATED BY:** Jock Willis Shipping Line
» **LAUNCHED:** November 1869
» **RETIRED:** December 1954
» **CREW:** 28–35
» **POWERED BY:** 2,973 m² of canvas sail
» **TOP SPEED:** 32.4 kph
» **CARGOES CARRIED:** Tea, alcohol and wool
» **DIMENSIONS:** Length: 65 m; Width (or 'Beam'): 11 m; Draft: 6.4 m; Height (tallest mast): 46 m

HOW THE TEA CLIPPER CHANGED THE WORLD

Tea clippers were the fastest commercial sailing ships ever built. Captains said that even at top speed *Cutty Sark* hardly disturbed the sea, and she once travelled 672 kilometres in only 24 hours. These ships carried valuable cargo like tea, wool and gold in record times, with people reading newspaper reports to see if their favourite clipper was winning the race from China. *Cutty Sark* is now preserved as a museum you can visit in Greenwich, close to where she used to arrive in front of cheering crowds, all those years ago.

SLIM HULLS, STUDDING SAILS AND MOONRAKERS

Cutty Sark has a 'composite hull', which is a wooden outer hull built around a wrought-iron frame. This made her strong and rigid enough to cope with long sea voyages, and lightweight so she could sail quickly. Older cargo ships were wide and heavy – built to carry bulk. Clippers were sleek and graceful, with narrow, streamlined hulls and sharp prows to cut through waves. Three masts tower over *Cutty Sark*'s deck, with her main mast presenting six sails; captains kept them raised even when gales pushed the vessel hard over, trusting her timbers to see them through to the finish line.

WHAT'S IN A NAME?

To 'clip along' or 'move at a clip' means to travel quickly, so these fast ships were called 'clippers'. They became famous, and everyone knew the names *Thermopylae*, *Ariel*, *Fiery Cross* and *Taeping* for their speed runs over the sea. The name *Cutty Sark* was taken from a poem by Robert Burns called 'Tam o' Shanter'. It tells the tale of Tam who, when riding home on his horse called Meg, stumbles upon a coven of witches. The witches chase him, and the one in front – who's wearing a dress called a 'cutty sark' – manages to pull off Meg's tail before Tam escapes. *Cutty Sark*'s figurehead is of that very witch as she brandishes poor Meg's tail.

FIRE ENGINE
EMERGENCY RESPONSE VEHICLE

Fire has been our friend for thousands of years. It has cooked our food, and lit and heated our homes. But it is also one of the most destructive forces on the planet, capable of burning entire forests and towns to ash. Fire spreads quickly, devouring everything within reach, and swift action is needed to prevent it from getting out of control. The first fire engines that allowed firefighters to reach and tackle blazes quickly were drawn by brave horses, some of which became famous in their local areas.

FACTS AND STATS

» **MODEL:** 1000 gallon 'double vertical' steam fire engine
» **BUILT BY:** Shand Mason, UK
» **LAUNCHED:** 1889
» **CREW:** 5–6 firefighters
» **POWERED BY:** 2 horses
» **AVERAGE SPEED:** 10–16 kph
» **PUMPING CAPACITY:** 4,500 lpm
» **DIMENSIONS:** Length: 4.42 m; Width: 2 m; Height: 2.6 m; Height of water jet: 62 m

CITIES TURN TO CINDERS

City-dwellers in the 17th century were terrified of fire – and with good reason. In January 1608, fire burned the US city of Virginia to the ground. In September 1666, the Great Fire of London utterly destroyed the central portion of the city. It only took a single stray spark from an untended fire to set thatched wooden buildings ablaze. Wardens were employed to raise the alarm and order people to form water-bucket lines to put out fires, but the first organised fire brigades did not appear until the next century.

SHAND MASON STEAM FIRE PUMP

London-based Shand Mason was one of the first companies to build fire engines. They were actually horse-drawn steam-powered pumps that directed strong, steady jets of water from a hose – perfect for dousing flames on the ground or higher up. When the alarm was raised, firefighters harnessed the horses, leaped on board and set off – lighting the hearth beneath the boiler even as they galloped along at top speed, and ringing a bell to warn people of their approach. When they reached the fire they unharnessed the horses, connected the hoses to the pumps and set to work.

FIRE HORSES

Horses chosen to pull fire engines were special and had to be strong, obedient, swift and fearless. Some were so intelligent they positioned themselves in front of the engine as soon as they heard the alarm. When they reached the fire, a good fire horse stayed calm even as people screamed, fires blazed, sparks flew, buildings collapsed and smoke billowed all around them. They took two years to train, and the strain of the job meant they only worked for about four years.

MODERN FIRE ENGINES

The first fire engines were hauled by people, then horses, then steam. Modern fire engines are petrol or diesel-powered trucks that carry everything firefighters need to tackle emergencies: floodlights, fire extinguishers, hoses, pumps, 'deluge guns' to spray water, rotatable and extendable ladders to rescue people from upper floors, and hydraulic tools to cut people out of wreckage. Their sirens, bright colours and flashing lights warn people to get out of the way.

HOW THE FIRE ENGINE CHANGED THE WORLD

Three hundred years ago, before fire brigades, firefighters and fire engines, people had to deal with dangerous blazes with little guidance, no training and no equipment except buckets and simple hand-powered water pumps. Everything changed with the introduction of professional firefighters using specialist equipment, and it's impossible to calculate how many lives firefighters and their trusty fire engines have saved over the centuries.

AUTOMOBILE
MASS-PRODUCED MOBILITY

Most automobiles in the early 1900s were unreliable and too expensive for ordinary people to afford. Henry Ford, an American industrialist, wanted to change this: "I will build a motor car for the great multitude. Large enough for the family . . . constructed of the best materials . . . but so low in price that anyone earning a good salary will be able to afford one – and enjoy the blessing of hours of pleasure in God's great open spaces." And so he and his team of engineers designed the iconic and world-changing Ford Model T.

A REVOLUTION BEGINS

The first automobile – a road-travelling vehicle powered by an internal combustion engine – was invented by German engineer Karl Benz in 1885. He called it the 'Motorwagen'. It was powered by a three-horsepower petrol engine of his own design, ran on three spoked wheels with solid rubber tyres, and had one forward gear. In 1888, Benz's wife, Bertha, undertook the very first long-distance road trip in an automobile when she drove a Motorwagen on a 194-kilometre round trip.

FACTS AND STATS

- » **AUTOMOBILE NAME:** Model T
- » **PICTURED TYPE:** 4-door touring car
- » **OTHER TYPES:** Speedster; Tudor sedan; Roadster; Tourabout; Runabout
- » **MANUFACTURED BY:** Ford Motor Company, USA
- » **MANUFACTURED BETWEEN:** 1908–1927
- » **NUMBER BUILT:** 15 million
- » **PASSENGERS:** 4–5 (including driver)
- » **POWERED BY:** 20 hp 4-cylinder engine
- » **FUELLED BY:** Petrol, kerosene or ethanol
- » **TOP SPEED:** 68 kph
- » **NUMBER OF GEARS:** 3 (2 forward, 1 reverse)
- » **DIMENSIONS:** Length: 3.4 m; Width: 1.7 m; Height: 1.9 m; Weight: 700 kg

NOT JUST A CAR

Henry Ford did not just create a family car – his Model T was designed to be used for lots of jobs. Almost any type of vehicle could be built on top of the Model T's chassis and engine: two-seater 'Runabouts', enclosed sedans, flatbed trucks, delivery vans, police cars, firefighter transport – they could even pull farm equipment like ploughs or be adapted into 'Snowflyers' to travel across snow. The Model T's incredible versatility made even more people want to buy it.

MASS PRODUCTION

Henry Ford's quest for an affordable car meant he had to produce them as cheaply as possible. To do this he created the 'moving assembly line'. First, each piece of the automobile was made by a machine. As the car's base, the chassis, moved along a conveyor belt, each piece (engine, wheel, window, etc) was attached by a skilled factory worker; a bare chassis was turned into a painted, fully functional automobile, all ready to be sold in just 1 hour 33 minutes, eight times faster than before. By 1925, around 10,000 Model Ts a day were rolling out of the factories.

CHEAP AND TRUSTWORTHY

Henry Ford wanted to turn the automobile from an expensive luxury into something anyone could afford. However, his Model T was an immediate success in America not just because it was cheap, but because it was a very good motor car. The engine was reliable, but also simple enough to be fixed if the owner knew what they were doing; the body was built from vanadium steel, which was both lightweight and strong; and the air-filled tyres and high chassis meant it travelled well over rough tracks. Before long, they were being built and sold all over the world.

HOW THE AUTOMOBILE CHANGED THE WORLD

Karl Benz built about 30 Motorwagens in the late 1800s; 15 million Model Ts rolled off Henry Ford's revolutionary moving production lines in the early 1900s, and now there are almost one and a half billion automobiles on the roads. These vehicles have changed our world and our lives. If people live far from work, friends or the shops, or want to take their family on a trip somewhere, they can simply hop in their car and go. The automobile has given billions of people far greater freedom, and opened up more leisure and work opportunities than at any other time in our history.

WRIGHT FLYER
MAGNIFICENT MEN IN THEIR FLYING MACHINE

On 17 December 1903, on the flat and sandy Outer Banks of North Carolina, USA, Orville Wright made history by leaving the ground at the controls of the first powered, heavier-than-air aeroplane: the *Flyer*. With its tiny engine buzzing, and propellers whirling, he guided the aeroplane into the air as his brother Wilbur ran alongside. The four flights they made that day were short, low, straight and ended with heavy landings, but they marked the moment that humans began their conquest of the skies – and beyond.

FACTS AND STATS

» **AIRCRAFT NAME:** *Wright Flyer* (also *Flyer 1*)

» **DESIGNED AND BUILT BY:** Wilbur and Orville Wright

» **DAY OF FLIGHTS:** 17 December 1903

» **LOCATION OF FLIGHTS:** Kitty Hawk, North Carolina, USA

» **NUMBER OF FLIGHTS:** 4

» **TOTAL DISTANCE TRAVELLED:** 411 m

» **CREW:** 1

» **POWERED BY:** 4-cylinder petrol engine (specially designed)

» **TOP SPEED:** 48 kph

» **DIMENSIONS:** Length: 6.4 m; Wingspan: 12.3 m; Height: 2.46 m; Weight: 274 kg

THE WRIGHT BROTHERS

From an early age, Americans Wilbur and Orville Wright were fascinated with the idea of flying. The brothers designed bicycles, which they sold in their own shop, before moving on to kites and gliders. The many tests they did made them realise that the secret to successful flight was having complete control of an aircraft's movement (pitch, roll and yaw), from take-off to landing. From there, they created their epoch-shattering *Flyer*.

LAUNCHING RAIL

To take off, the *Flyer* trundled down an 18-metre wooden rail on a detachable wheeled trolley. Landing was less controlled, even on the flat, sandy surface; the fourth and last landing on that historic day damaged the elevator and the *Flyer* never took off again.

STRUTS

The struts were movable to allow the wings to adjust their shape ('warping') when the pilot shifted the hip cradle; the *Flyer* rolled when the wings warped.

RIGGING

Bicycle-spoke wire was attached diagonally between the struts to keep the airframe rigid and airworthy.

AIRFRAME

The airframe was made from spruce and ash trees – strong woods that were also flexible and able to absorb shocks during a heavy landing.

PROPELLERS

The Wright brothers realised that flat, curved propellers created lots of 'thrust', which would push their aircraft forward and lift it into the air. Each propeller was 243 centimetres long, spun in opposite directions so the plane flew in a straight line, and was connected to the engine crankshaft with a bicycle chain.

A COAT OF PAINT

The wings, elevators and rudders were tightly covered in cotton muslin, which was stiffened and strengthened with special paint.

ELEVATOR

The elevator changed the aircraft's 'pitch' (the angle of flight). Pulling back on the wooden control stick made the plane go 'up'; pushing forward made the plane go 'down'.

HIP CRADLE

The pilot lay on their front in the hip cradle, which they moved from side to side by shifting their hips left and right. This action tipped the wings (causing the plane to turn in a 'bank' or 'roll') and moved the rudder (causing the plane to 'yaw', or change direction).

ENGINE

Orville, Wilbur and a mechanic called Charlie Taylor designed and built their own aluminium and copper petrol engine. It was light (only 82 kilograms) but powerful enough (12 horsepower) to get *Flyer* into the air. There was no throttle – the engine was either 'on' or 'off'.

HOW THE WRIGHT FLYER CHANGED THE WORLD

The Wright brothers continued to improve on the *Flyer* design, and soon other engineers were using Wilbur and Orville's ideas to make ever more advanced aircraft: the first trip around the world (a 'circumnavigation') in an aircraft occurred only 21 years later in 1924; rocket and jet planes were streaking through the skies by the 1940s, and in 1969 humans reached the Moon. None of this would have happened without the visionary genius and hard work of Wilbur and Orville Wright.

OCEAN LINER
QUEENS OF THE SEA

In 1907, the White Star Line shipping company decided to build the three most luxurious ocean liners ever put to sea: the RMSs *Titanic, Britannic* and *Olympic*. With their elegant steel hulls and towering funnels, these liners were the envy of the world. Passengers could stroll the decks, take tea, breathe in the sea breeze and enjoy the very best food and facilities. Although designed to serve for many years, two of these magnificent ships were sadly destined for tragedy.

FOOD, GLORIOUS FOOD

On board were 60 cooks, 14 butchers and 20 bakers who worked all hours to prepare thousands of meals every day. First-class passengers enjoyed lavish food such as steak, lobster, shrimp, oysters, poached salmon, roast duck, puddings and French ice cream. Third-class meals were simpler but still tasty: smoked herring, ham and eggs for breakfast; roast beef, potatoes and plum pudding for lunch; and cold meats and cheese for supper.

LUXURIOUS LINERS

Olympic-class liners were the largest machines in the world at that time, and were fitted out with all sorts of luxurious facilities: a Turkish bath complete with sauna, steam and cooling rooms; a fully equipped gymnasium, a swimming pool and a squash court, with a professional player on hand for lessons; lounges where passengers could mingle and drink tea; and writing rooms to write letters and postcards.

FACTS AND STATS

» **CLASS:** Olympic
» **VESSEL NAME:** RMS (Royal Mail Ship) *Olympic*
» **BUILT BY:** Harland & Wolff, Northern Ireland
» **OWNED BY:** White Star Line
» **SERVICE LIFE:** 1911–1935
» **CREW:** 900 (approx.)
» **PASSENGERS:** 2,400
» **POWERED BY:** 2 x 4-cylinder engines and 1 steam turbine
» **COMBINED ENGINE POWER:** 50,000 hp
» **TOP SPEED:** 43 kph
» **TONNAGE:** 46,000
» **DIMENSIONS:** Length: 269 m; Width (or 'Beam'): 28 m; Height (keel to top of funnels): 53.4 m; Draught: 10.5 m

A GRAND DECEPTION

Funnels were used to get rid of all the smoke and excess steam produced by the huge, engine-driving boilers. However, Olympic-class liners only used three of their four funnels for this purpose; the funnel at the back was actually a dummy, added to make the ship look larger and extra grand.

UNLUCKY SISTERS

The *Olympic* had two famous sister ships, the *Titanic* and *Britannic*. After setting sail on her maiden voyage in April 1912, the *Titanic* scraped against an iceberg and began to sink. Two and a half hours later, with her stern pointing up at the night sky, she slid beneath the waves and disappeared. Of the 2,208 people on board, only 705 survived. The *Britannic* was converted into a hospital ship during the First World War. In 1916, she struck a mine in the Mediterranean Sea and sank less than an hour later, taking 30 people down with her.

WHITE STAR LINE

CLASS SYSTEM

The three classes of passenger each had their own areas on the ship. First-class passengers enjoyed spacious suites with private bathrooms, easy access to the open decks, and luxurious lounges filled with the finest furniture and fittings. Second-class passengers had their own smoking room, library and lift. Third-class passengers lived in the lower decks. Although their cabins were small, they were better than the shared dormitories on other ocean liners at that time.

HOW THE OCEAN LINER CHANGED THE WORLD

These ocean giants allowed people to voyage quickly and safely all over the world. Although built with luxury in mind, ships like the *Olympic* also gave less wealthy people the opportunity to travel to other countries for an affordable price. It wasn't until the invention of the commercial jet airliner (see page 86) that the ocean liner's golden age came to an end.

OMNIBUS
DOUBLE-DECKER TRANSPORT

In 1910, a new vehicle appeared on the busy streets of London. Bright red, double-decked and puttering along on solid rubber tyres, the LGOC B-type motorised omnibus stood out among the horse-drawn carriages and carts. Covered in adverts and carrying passengers on fixed routes, they were an immediate success – by 1914, there were 2,500 B-types serving the city. Since then, the scarlet London bus has become iconic – recognised the world over as a symbol of Great Britain.

MUSCLE BEFORE MOTORS

The first omnibuses were horse-drawn and appeared in England and France during the 1820s. These large, four-wheeled and sometimes double-decked carriages ran on planned routes and allowed paying passengers to hop on board without needing to book a ticket in advance. This cheap and convenient service was incredibly popular, and soon many more omnibus companies were popping up all over Europe.

THE LGOC B-TYPE

Designed by engineer Frank Searle, the B-type was the first mass-produced motorised omnibus in the world. The frame was made from wood, which made it strong but lightweight, and the chassis and wheelbase from steel. After buying a ticket from the conductor, passengers could sit in the sheltered lower deck, or climb upstairs to enjoy the view. The motor (started by the driver turning a handle at the front) could run the omnibus all day – a great improvement on horse-drawn omnibuses, which had to regularly rest, feed and replace their horses.

FACTS AND STATS

- » **CLASS:** B-type
- » **DESIGNED BY:** Frank Searle
- » **BUILT AND OPERATED BY:** London General Omnibus Company, UK
- » **PRODUCED BETWEEN:** 1910–1914
- » **NUMBER BUILT:** 2,500
- » **CREW:** 2 (driver and conductor)
- » **PASSENGERS:** 34 (16 downstairs and 18 upstairs)
- » **POWERED BY:** 52 hp 4-cylinder petrol engine
- » **TOP SPEED:** 26 kph
- » **DIMENSIONS:** Length: 7 m; Width: 2 m; Height: 4 m

ALL ABOARD FOR THE WESTERN FRONT

Because the B-type was so reliable, the British War Office (what we now call the Ministry of Defence) used 900 of them on the Western Front as troop transports during the First World War – they even kept their bright red colour and adverts for a while, until it was painted over with camouflage. With the lower-deck windows boarded up, the B-type could carry 25 soldiers and their equipment; some were even converted into mobile Carrier pigeon coops. These sturdy omnibuses served throughout the whole war, with their final duty being to bring the troops back home.

MODERN BUSES

Ever since the B-type carried its first passenger load through the foggy roads of Edwardian London, the motorised omnibus – more commonly called the 'bus' – has been used all over the world as a safe and affordable way for people to go about their daily business. Modern designs come in all shapes and sizes, from little local buses, to double-deckers, to long, articulated (or 'bendy') buses, and are often equipped with ramps to allow easy access for wheelchair users. Most have diesel engines, but more are now being built to run on eco-friendly fuels such as electricity, hydrogen, natural gas and biodiesel.

HOW THE OMNIBUS CHANGED THE WORLD

The mass-produced motorised omnibus has had a huge effect on the world. In the first half of the 1900s, when most people did not have their own form of transport, omnibuses provided the means for them to reach beyond their local neighbourhoods – to socialise, find work and discover new opportunities. Even today, in the age of the automobile, buses are still a vital way to keep people and communities connected.

TANK
ARMOURED BEASTS OF THE BATTLEFIELD

By 1915, soldiers in the First World War couldn't cross the muddy, shell-hole-strewn battlefields without being decimated by machine guns or caught on barbed wire. A vehicle had to be invented to batter through obstacles and create a path towards the enemy trenches: a cross between an armoured fortress and a steel battering ram, bulletproof and bristling with guns. And so it was that the tank was born from the nightmare of no man's land.

FACTS AND STATS

- » **TANK TYPE:** British Army Mark IV
- » **BUILT BETWEEN:** 1917–1918
- » **NUMBER BUILT:** 1,222
- » **CREW:** 8
- » **POWERED BY:** 105 hp Foster-Daimler 6-cylinder petrol engine
- » **TOP SPEED:** 5.6 kph (over level ground)
- » **RANGE:** 24 km (over level ground)
- » **ARMOUR THICKNESS:** 12 mm (front); 8 mm (side); 6 mm (rear)
- » **ARMAMENT:** 2 x 6-pounder guns and 3 x light machine guns
- » **DIMENSIONS:** Length: 8 m; Width: 4.1 m; Height: 2.5 m; Weight: 30 tonnes

CARRIER PIGEONS

Many tanks had homing Carrier pigeons in wicker baskets. To send a message back to base, the commander placed it in a metal cylinder on the pigeon's back, and let the bird go through one of the windows. The pigeon then flew off and (with a bit of luck) delivered the message.

A SECRET WEAPON

The tank was a brand-new vehicle that the British hoped would help them win the war, and it was vital to keep it secret during development in 1915. They were referred to as 'water tanks' on all the paperwork to keep their true purpose hidden from enemy spies. The name 'tank' stuck, and eventually became official.

CATERPILLAR TRACKS

Tank designers soon realised that caterpillar tracks like those used on farm tractors were the only way for heavy vehicles to move across the mud and mire of no man's land. They provided maximum grip on slopes and slippery surfaces, and allowed the tank to cross trenches to get behind enemy lines.

A NOISY AND POISONOUS OVEN

Conditions inside were terrible: it was cramped, noisy and smelly. Crews were deafened by the engine and the roar of their own guns, roasted by red-hot exhaust pipes, sickened and suffocated by gun smoke and poisonous fumes, terrified by enemy bullets smacking into the armour, and knocked about by the tank's constant pitching and lurching.

HOW THE TANK CHANGED THE WORLD

The invention of tanks allowed armies to break through enemy defences, so that the fighting infantry could advance more safely through the gap. After the First World War, tanks got faster, more reliable and carried bigger guns that could be accurately aimed. As well as being weapons, modern tanks can also clear minefields, transport troops, tow heavy equipment and lay bridges.

ARMOUR

The Mark IV was covered in steel armour, thickest at the front because that was where most enemy gunfire would hit. It was strong enough to protect the crew from rifle and machine-gun bullets but not an explosive shell fired by a long-range field gun.

TURNING A TANK

Changing direction needed the cooperation of the whole crew (except the gunners). First, the commander got their attention by banging a spanner against the metalwork. Then he used hand signals to indicate which direction he wanted to turn. A gearsman pulled a lever to stop one of the tracks; the other still-moving track pushed the tank in the direction the commander wanted it to go.

WEAPONS

This version of the Mark IV was armed with three light machine guns and two six-pounder guns. When the tank was being transported by train, the gun turrets (called 'sponsons') could be pushed inside to save space. Tank crews were trained by the Royal Navy because aiming and firing a gun from a tank moving on uneven ground was similar to doing so from a ship pitching and rolling at sea.

AMBULANCE
EMERGENCY RESPONSE

These days, many people are lucky enough to know that if they are badly injured or become seriously unwell, a fully equipped ambulance driven by paramedics is only a phone call away. The internal combustion engine made vehicles like this possible, but it was many decades before ambulances became the life-saving mobile hospitals that we see today. One of the first ambulances ever built was the Ford M1917, which was used during the First World War.

THE MEDICAL MODEL T

The Ford Model T (see page 36) wheelbase and chassis were designed to be used for many vehicle types, not just regular automobiles. By building a fully enclosed wooden compartment behind the driver's seat, complete with a bed, benches and large rear door, it proved itself to be a reliable ambulance capable of tackling the muddy, rough terrain of the First World War's battlefields. There was no medical equipment on board (only stretchers, blankets and pillows), and the drivers and crew (many of whom were female volunteers) were not usually medically trained – the M1917's job was simply to transport the wounded as quickly as possible to the nearest field hospital.

FACTS AND STATS

- » **AMBULANCE NAME:** M1917
- » **MANUFACTURED BY:** Ford, USA
- » **NUMBER BUILT:** 20,700
- » **CREW:** 2
- » **POWERED BY:** 20 hp 4-cylinder Ford L-head engine
- » **FUEL TYPE:** Petrol
- » **TOP SPEED:** 68 kph
- » **GEARS:** 2
- » **DIMENSIONS:** Length: 3.4 m; Width: 1.7 m; Weight: 700 kg

COURAGEOUS CREWS

During wartime, it is illegal to open fire on ambulances and their crew. This is because they are classed as 'non-combatants' – meaning they are not armed and are not involved in the actual fighting. To ensure the enemy knows not to attack, ambulances are clearly marked with a red cross on a white background, the emblem of the Red Cross. However, this doesn't protect these brave ambulance crews from being accidentally targeted or caught in a crossfire.

MODERN AMBULANCES

Modern ambulances do not just carry patients to hospitals like the M1917s did – they are equipped to provide medical care as soon as they arrive on the scene and during the journey back. The two-person crew are usually paramedics trained to cope with all kinds of emergencies and accidents. The inside of the ambulance is like a mini hospital, with all sorts of equipment such as a defibrillator to monitor a patient's heartbeat, oxygen cylinders and masks, splints for broken bones, bandages, pads and antiseptic wipes.

BIGGER, BETTER, BRIGHTER

The ambulances we see on the roads these days are very different from the M1917 – they are larger, faster, more reliable and much better equipped. However, just like how the M1917 was a specially adapted Ford Model T, modern ambulances are also often adapted from standard vans or light trucks; the back of the ambulance – where the patient, paramedics and all the emergency medical equipment are kept – is built separately and then attached to the van or truck chassis. Bright colours, reflective panels, flashing lights and sirens warn people that an ambulance is coming – and to get out of the way.

HOW THE AMBULANCE CHANGED THE WORLD

When someone is hurt or suffering a severe health crisis, it is incredibly important for doctors to get to them quickly. Even a short delay in receiving medical help can mean the difference between life and death. During both war and peace, ambulances like the M1917 were vital in transporting the wounded to hospitals where they could be treated. Modern ambulances, fully equipped and crewed by medical professionals, are even more effective lifesavers, because they can deal with the patient as soon as they arrive. They are a vital part of the modern world, and we are lucky to have them and their crews.

RIGID AIRSHIP
THE FIRST AIRLINERS

During her first record-breaking flight to America, the rigid airship *Graf Zeppelin* was nearly destroyed in a storm. However, skilfully captained by her inventor, Dr Hugo Eckener, she arrived safely over New York to huge excitement. Soon afterwards, these gas-filled giants were regularly carrying people across the Atlantic – and in luxury too. Passengers slept in private cabins, ate delicious food from china plates, and marvelled at the incredible views of land and sea drifting by below.

WEAPON OF WAR

Rigid airships were used during the First World War to spot enemy ships and carry out air raids. Airships flew high to avoid fighter planes, but this made hitting their targets with bombs difficult.

D-LZ127

FACTS AND STATS

- » AIRSHIP NAME: LZ 127 *Graf Zeppelin*
- » BUILT BY: Luftschiffbau Zeppelin, Germany
- » NUMBER OF FLIGHTS: 590
- » TOTAL FLIGHT TIME: 17,177 hours
- » ERA OF DOMINANCE: 1928–1937
- » CREW: 36
- » PASSENGERS: 24
- » POWERED BY: 5 x 550 hp Maybach VL II propeller engines
- » TOP SPEED: 128 kph
- » RANGE: 10,000 km
- » DIMENSIONS: Length: 236.6 m; Width (or 'Beam'): 30.5 m; Height: 33.5 m

ENGINES

Five propeller engines pushed the *Graf Zeppelin* through the skies. They were fitted inside streamlined cases called 'nacelles'. The engines were mostly fuelled by blau gas, which is only slightly heavier than air. This meant that the airship's overall weight didn't change much as the gas was used up (unlike with heavier petrol), making it easier to maintain level flight.

GASBAGS

Inside the frame and envelope were 17 cells (large bags) filled with lighter-than-air hydrogen gas – this is what gave the airship the 'lift' it needed to float above the ground. Each hydrogen cell was made from processed animal intestines, and together contained 75,000 square metres of gas. Hydrogen had to be handled with care – it would only take a single spark to set it ablaze.

FRAME

A rigid metal frame of rings and struts (or 'girders') made from duralumin (a mixture of aluminium and copper) gave the airship its shape. The thick cotton fabric that covered the frame (called the 'envelope') was covered with a liquid which hardened and made it waterproof.

HOW THE RIGID AIRSHIP CHANGED THE WORLD

For the first three decades of the 20th century, rigid airships allowed people to travel to faraway destinations in relative comfort; journeys that might take weeks by ship or train were completed in a matter of days – at least for those rich enough to afford it. However, the tragic fate of LZ 129 *Hindenburg* changed everything. On 6 May 1937, a blaze, possibly caused by leaking hydrogen, destroyed her and killed 35 people in a matter of seconds. Caught on film, this disaster showed the world how vulnerable airships were to fire, and their golden age was over.

BALLAST TANKS

If the airship began to lose height, water stored in tanks (called 'ballast') was dumped into the air. This made the airship lighter and allowed it to climb higher into the sky. Airships like the *Graf Zeppelin* usually cruised at about 200 metres (that's 35 metres lower than Canary Wharf in London), but flew higher to avoid bad weather.

EATING

Three hot meals a day were prepared in the kitchen. The menu included turkey, lobster, French fries, caviar (fish eggs), bread, butter, eggs, frankfurter sausages, ice cream and fruit. Passengers gathered in the dining room and lounge to eat, socialise, and watch the landscape and clouds pass by through four large windows.

CABINS

Cabins slept two, and during the day they could be converted into a living space, complete with sofa. Separate washrooms and chemical toilets were found at the end of the corridor.

GRAF ZEPPELIN

GONDOLA

The 30-metre-long gondola was where the crew controlled the airship, and the passengers passed the time on their journey. Although luxurious, the gondola was unheated, so passengers sometimes had to wear winter coats, gloves and scarfs to keep warm.

CONTROL ROOM

The airship was flown from the control room. Nearby was a map room for navigation, and a radio room for communication. A ladder in the map room led up into the frame, where the crew quarters were located.

BUSH AEROPLANE
LIGHTWEIGHT LIFESAVERS

Before the 1930s, people living in the vast wilderness of the Australian Outback stood little chance of survival if they became seriously ill or injured – hospitals were simply too far away to reach in time by road. This changed in 1928 with the introduction of the Flying Doctors, who have since saved countless lives. Speeding to the rescue in their tough little bush aeroplanes, they can touch down on the roughest of landing spots, bring the patient on board and take off again in a matter of minutes.

FACTS AND STATS

» **AIRCRAFT NAME:** DH.83 Fox Moth
» **MANUFACTURED BY:** de Havilland Aircraft Company, UK
» **FIRST FLIGHT:** March 1932
» **NUMBER BUILT:** 153
» **CREW:** 1 pilot
» **PASSENGERS:** 3–4
» **POWERED BY:** Single 130 hp 4-cylinder Gipsy IIIA engine
» **TOP SPEED:** 171 kph
» **RANGE:** 684 km
» **MAX ALTITUDE:** 3,900 m
» **DIMENSIONS:** Length: 7.8 m; Wingspan: 9.4 m; Height: 2.7 m

WINGED RESCUE

The Australian Flying Doctor Service needed reliable aircraft that were easy to maintain, could travel long distances, accommodate a pilot and a doctor or nurse as well as a patient on a stretcher, and be able to land and take off from the short, dusty airstrips found in the Outback. Built from sturdy wood and plywood, with strong wheels capable of surviving heavy landings, and space for a stretcher inside an enclosed cabin, the de Havilland DH.83 Fox Moth was one of the first aircraft to fit the bill and was successfully used throughout the 1930s and 1940s.

HOW THE BUSH AEROPLANE CHANGED THE WORLD

For about a century, bush aeroplanes like the Fox Moth have made life for people living in the world's most remote places safer and more secure. Their combination of lightness, strength and carrying capacity means they can fly quickly, cope with poor weather conditions, and land on short airstrips, water or snow, while carrying passengers, cargo, life-saving equipment and provisions, or people desperate for medical attention. It's impossible to estimate just how many lives have been saved by bush aeroplanes.

THE SUGAR BIRD LADY

One of the most amazing Flying Doctors was a woman called Robin Miller Dicks. In the 1960s, a career flying planes was not considered appropriate for a woman. However, Robin trained as a nurse and pilot, bought her own plane, and flew all over the Outback to vaccinate 37,000 children against a disease called polio. The children called her the Sugar Bird Lady, because she administered the vaccine inside sugar lumps. Afterwards, Robin joined the Flying Doctor Service and, unlike most of the male pilots, could fly her plane solo, treat the patients herself (she once delivered a baby in the back seat of her airborne plane), and make her own repairs. She was a life-saving pioneer who left a bright trail in the sky for other nurses to follow.

MODERN BUSH AEROPLANES

Bush aeroplanes such as the Cessna Caravan or Quest Kodiak are still used all over the world to ferry people and cargo to remote locations, carry out rescue operations and deal with medical emergencies. Although their designs vary, bush aeroplanes share certain characteristics: most are Short Take-Off and Landing (STOL) vehicles; they can be fitted with skis for snow landings or floats for water landings; high wings make it easier to load and unload cargo, people or patients; large, soft tyres enable the pilot to land on rough ground if there's no landing strip; and they have simple piston engines that can be more easily maintained and repaired when out in the wilderness.

COMBINE HARVESTER
THE REAPING, THRESHING AND WINNOWING WONDER

From the moment they began growing wheat, barley and rye fields to feed their families thousands of years ago, the first farmers knew that the autumn harvest was an important time. As soon as the crops were golden and rustled dryly in the breeze, they had to be gathered in before disease or heavy rain spoiled them. Failure to harvest properly or at the right time led to food shortages, malnutrition and starvation. For centuries this vital job was done slowly by hand. Nowadays we use machines, and the most important is the combine harvester.

HAND REAPING

For centuries crops were harvested by hand (and still are today in some places). The tops of the crop – the edible 'ears' – could be plucked off and dropped in a basket, ready to be processed into flour. Or the whole stalk was cut near the base by a crescent-shaped blade with a short handle called a 'sickle', or a straighter blade with a much longer handle called a 'scythe'. The stalks were bundled together into sheaves, dried out, and then 'threshed' with a tool called a 'flail' (two long sticks attached to each other by a chain) to separate the grain from the straw. It took a lot of time and effort to hand-reap a field, and when finished the whole community celebrated with a harvest festival.

FACTS AND STATS

- » **MODEL NAME:** MH-20
- » **MANUFACTURED BY:** Massey-Harris, USA
- » **LAUNCHED:** 1938
- » **NUMBER BUILT:** 1,000
- » **CREW:** 1 driver
- » **TOP SPEED:** 20 kph
- » **DIMENSIONS:** Length: 3.4 m; Width: 5.2 m; Height: 3.4 m

HARVESTING MACHINES

From the late 1700s, machines were invented to do the various harvesting jobs. Horse-drawn 'reapers' cut the crops as they moved across the field, and some (called 'reaper-binders') also tied it into sheaves. 'Threshers' – powered by hand and then by steam engine – beat the crops to separate the grain from the stalk. These machines completely changed the way farms worked by removing the need to have dozens of harvest workers doing hours of boring labour. However, each machine only completed one part of the whole process – the farmers' dream was to have one machine that could do it all.

THE FIRST COMBINE HARVESTERS

Combine harvesters are machines that reap, thresh, gather and winnow (separate the grain from the useless husk) the crops all at the same time. The first combine harvesters were huge contraptions that needed a crew of workers to operate and teams of up to 20 horses or mules to pull; by the early 1900s they were being hauled by tractors. However, the first self-propelled combine harvester (with a petrol engine driving both the wheels and the harvesting mechanism) was the Massey-Harris MH-20, an all-in-one harvesting machine that only needed one person to operate. The design was perfected in the next model, the MH-21, which was lighter, cheaper and sold in the tens of thousands.

MASSEY-
HARRIS

HOW THE COMBINE HARVESTER CHANGED THE WORLD

The Massey-Harris MH-20 and its single operator could do in one day what a whole team of workers needed weeks to do by hand. Its ingenious design laid the foundation of every other combine since its introduction in 1938. Combine harvesters save huge amounts of time and effort in the vital work of growing our food. In 2021, the record amount of 2,791 million tonnes of cereal (including wheat, barley and oats) was grown and harvested worldwide – an impossibility without the world-changing combine harvester.

TRAM
TRACKS THROUGH TOWNS

The Portuguese city of Lisbon is an ancient place, and it's not just the buildings that are historic – so too is the 150-year-old tram network and the trundling Remodelado trams from the 1930s that run on it. The network also uses modern trams, but it's only the shorter, older models like this one that can make their way through the city's narrowest, hilliest and most windy streets. Despite their age, these clanking, screeching trams still faithfully serve the citizens and tourists of Lisbon.

TRAMS, STREETCARS AND TROLLEYS

Trams – also called 'streetcars' or 'trolleys' – are one of the earliest forms of mass public transport, providing a cheap and easy way to travel around urban areas. Unlike trains, trams follow tracks that have been built into city roads, meaning they run alongside cars and pedestrians with no separating barrier. Trams are lighter than trains, run on shorter routes and their stops are often positioned closer together.

HORSE-DRAWN TRAMS

The first passenger tram service was the nine-kilometre-long Swansea and Mumbles Railway in Wales, which opened in 1807, was hauled by horse, and ran on narrow tracks. Over the following decades, more tramlines appeared in Europe, the USA, South America, Africa and Asia. Using horses had drawbacks: they could only pull the tram for a few hours at a time, meaning tram companies had to use lots to ensure their lines operated properly; keeping all those horses fed, rested, groomed and healthy was expensive and time-consuming, and the huge amounts of manure they left on the streets had to be cleaned up.

FACTS AND STATS

» **TRAM NETWORK:** Lisbon Transport Network, Portugal
» **OPENED:** 1873
» **NUMBER OF ROUTES:** 6
» **TOTAL ROUTE LENGTH:** 26 km
» **PICTURED TRAM TYPE:** Remodelado
» **REMODELADO TRAM INTRODUCED:** 1932–1940
» **OTHER TRAM TYPE ON NETWORK:** Siemens Articulado
» **CREW:** 1 driver
» **POWERED BY:** 600-volt overhead cables
» **TOP SPEED:** 45 kph
» **TRACK GAUGE:** 90 cm
» **DIMENSIONS:** Length: 8.4 m; Width: 2.4 m

NEW METHODS OF MOTION

By the late 1800s most trams were powered by electricity. Poles called 'pantographs' on the tram's roof drew electricity from overhead wires, which was used to drive the wheel motors – most modern trams still work in this way. Some trams were pulled by small steam trains, however, the noise and smoke they produced was not welcome, and most were soon replaced by electric trams.

HAULING UP HILLS

In the early days, trams were not powerful enough to travel up steep slopes, which was a problem for the famously hilly city of San Francisco, USA. So a cable-car system was installed – three-centimetre-wide moving cables, situated just under the road's surface, pulled trams along the streets and up hills. To stop, the driver (called the 'grip') pulled a lever, which released the tram from the cable. Cable-car tram networks were built in other places too, including Australia, New Zealand, Germany and the UK.

HOW THE TRAM CHANGED THE WORLD

Trams like Lisbon's famous Remodelado have been in use all over the world for 200 years, providing city-dwellers with a reliable way to get about. The invention of the automobile (see page 36) and the omnibus (see page 42) led to many tram lines being shut down. However, from the 1980s, many cities (especially in Europe) have built new environmentally friendly tramways to reduce traffic congestion and help fight climate change.

MOTORCYCLE
TWO-WHEELED SPEEDSTERS

In 1885, a very strange vehicle with a single driver perched on a seat over a metal frame, two wheels and an engine, puttered its way down a road in Germany. People stopped and stared – they'd never seen anything like it before. It was called the Daimler 'Reitwagon' (which means 'riding car'), could reach a top speed of 11 kilometres per hour (which is actually quite slow), and was the first-ever petrol-driven bicycle. Since that day, millions of riders all over the world have fallen in love with the fast, agile and exciting motorcycle – despite the danger involved.

FACTS AND STATS

» **MOTORCYCLE NAME:** Sokół ('Falcon') 1000 M111

» **MANUFACTURED BY:** PZInż (National Engineering Works), Poland

» **BUILT BETWEEN:** 1933–1939

» **NUMBER BUILT:** 3,400

» **POWERED BY:** 18 hp 2-cylinder petrol V-45 engine

» **TOP SPEED:** 100 kph

» **GEARS:** 3

» **DIMENSIONS:** Length: 2.3 m (2.5 m with sidecar); Width: 0.8 m (1.7 m with sidecar); Height: 1.1 m; Weight: 270 kg (375 kg with sidecar)

FROM CYCLE TO MOTORCYCLE

The first self-propelled, two-wheeled vehicles appeared in the 1860s, and were bicycles fitted with small steam engines. They were experimental and ingenious, but too difficult to use to become popular. Next came motorbikes powered by small, petrol-driven engines, which were faster and more reliable. By the 1900s, lots of manufacturers were designing ever better motorcycles for thrill-seeking travellers to explore on.

MILITARY MOTORCYCLES

Tens of thousands of motorcycles, mostly manufactured by Harley Davidson, Indian and Triumph, were used during the First World War. Lightweight and speedy, they could travel over rough, war-torn terrain to deliver messages, transport wounded soldiers in sidecars, and explore enemy territory. The Sokół 1000 (pictured) was designed in the 1930s for the Polish Army, which wanted a reliable, durable machine that was easy to repair and could travel quickly off-road. Countries all over the world still use motorcycles in their armed forces.

SMALL AND NIMBLE

Cheap motorcycles with small engines are very popular in Asia, Africa and South America. The Honda Super Cub is the most produced motorcycle in history, and most of the 60 million made since 1958 were sold in the developing world. Motorcycles like the Super Cub, as well as mopeds and scooters, are often used as delivery vehicles and taxis (with the passenger sitting behind the driver) because they are perfect for zipping up alleyways and through streets that are choked with traffic. Riding motorcycles can be dangerous, so riders wear helmets and padded clothes to minimise injuries if they crash or fall off.

ELECTRIC MOTORBIKES

Like other vehicles in this book – such as the steam locomotive (see page 24), the automobile (see page 36) and the omnibus (see page 42) – motorbikes were first propelled by steam, then petrol, and are now moving rapidly towards becoming electrically powered. The speed and range of an electric motorbike is limited by the power capacity of the batteries used, and are not really comparable to petrol-powered machines. However, many companies are experimenting and designs are becoming more and more sophisticated. The future of motorcycles is electric.

HOW THE MOTORCYCLE CHANGED THE WORLD

Motorcycles have changed a lot since the Daimler Reitwagen first puttered down the road in Germany. Once they became reliable enough in the early 1900s, motorcycles began to take over from horses (especially in the military), and in the developing world are becoming as popular as the car. And they are still going strong today for work, sport and leisure, with new eco-friendly electric models getting faster and having longer ranges than ever before.

AIRCRAFT CARRIER
STEEL FORTRESSES OF THE SEA

Over 100 years ago, armies realised how useful it would be to have aeroplanes and helicopters parked at sea. It would help them to spot enemy vessels and to reach remote areas more quickly. So, in 1914, the British Royal Navy launched the HMS *Ark Royal*, the first specialised flat-decked aircraft carrier. Since then, these cities at sea have become ever bigger and more sophisticated, as demonstrated by the mighty Nimitz class.

FACTS AND STATS

- » **CLASS:** Nimitz
- » **VESSEL NAME:** USS *Harry S Truman*
- » **BUILT BY:** Newport News Shipbuilding Company, USA
- » **NUMBER OF CLASS BUILT:** 10
- » **LAUNCHED:** 1986
- » **CREW:** 558 officers, 5,454 crew
- » **POWERED BY:** 2 x 260,000 shp A4W nuclear reactors
- » **TOP SPEED:** 56 kph
- » **AIRCRAFT:** Max 130 x F18 Hornets, or 90 x various types
- » **DIMENSIONS:** Length: 333 m; Width (or 'Beam'): 78 m; Height: 74 m; Displacement: 104,000 tonnes; Draft: 11 m

CARRIER STRIKE FORCE

Although aircraft carriers have their own short-range defences, they are at risk of attack by aircraft, missiles or submarines. That is why they never travel alone. Instead, they sail as part of a Carrier Strike Force (CSF). These small fleets protect the carrier, and include a supply ship, military vessels called cruisers, destroyers and frigates, and at least one submarine.

NUCLEAR POWERED

Nimitz class carriers are powered by two A4W nuclear reactors, which use a fuel called uranium. A process called 'nuclear fission' heats up seawater, which creates steam. This steam spins four electricity-creating turbine machines. The energy produced by the turbines turns the four huge bronze propellers, and powers all of the ship's lights, pumps and electrical equipment.

FLOATING CITIES

It takes a huge effort to keep a crew of 6,000 hard-working men and women fed and looked after on voyages that can last many months. One hundred cooks produce around 17,000 meals every day in the seven galleys (kitchens), from first breakfast at 6 a.m. to midnight rations. There are gyms to keep the crew fit, and rooms for socialising, watching TV and playing games.

TAKE-OFF

Aircraft carriers are not long enough for planes to reach take-off speed without help, so they have to be launched off the deck. Planes are attached by their front wheel to one of four steam-powered catapults. Steam created by the nuclear reactors is fed into the catapult, which builds pressure. When pilots throttle their engine to maximum power the catapult is released, launching the plane from 0–275 kilometres per hour in only two seconds.

LANDING

Landing an aircraft on a moving carrier is extremely difficult and dangerous, especially at night or in rough seas. The pilot must approach the ship's stern at the correct angle and speed, then hit the deck with the aircraft positioned nose-up/tail-down. If done properly, a tailhook dangling from the plane snags one of four 'arrestor' cables stretched across the deck. These cables slow the plane down from 240 kilometres per hour to a full stop in two seconds. If the pilot misses the cables, they must put full power back into their engine and take off again – this is called a 'bolter'.

HOW THE AIRCRAFT CARRIER CHANGED THE WORLD

The seas were once ruled by battleships (see page 20) – vast vessels bristling with guns and protected by armour – but the invention and development of the aircraft carrier during the 20th century made them unnecessary. Nowadays, carriers allow nations to patrol, protect and if needs be launch attacks at sea or inland, anywhere in the world. They can also speed to places struck by earthquakes, hurricanes, floods or tsunamis to help with rescue operations.

TRACTOR
A FARMER'S BEST FRIEND

When you think of a farm, what images spring to mind? Red-roofed barns, hay bales, swaying fields of wheat – and the farmer's best friend, the tractor. With their huge wheels, deep treads and high chassis, tractors can work all year round, trundling along the muddiest tracks and over the roughest pastures with ease – modern farms simply wouldn't be able to function without them. One of the first successful tractors was the Ford 8N – a smart little red-and-grey revolution on wheels.

FACTS AND STATS

» **SERIES:** N-series
» **PICTURED MODEL:** 8N
» **OTHER MODELS:** 2N and 9N
» **MANUFACTURED BY:** Ford, USA
» **NUMBER BUILT:** 500,000+
» **DESIGNED BY:** Harry Ferguson
» **N-SERIES BUILT BETWEEN:** 1939–1952
» **POWERED BY:** 27 hp 4-cylinder petrol engine
» **TOP SPEED:** 25 kph
» **GEARS:** 4 forward, 1 reverse
» **DIMENSIONS:** Length: 2.9 m; Width: 1.6 m; Height: 1.4 m

THE FIRST FARMS

Farming is one of the most important developments in history. Many thousands of years ago in the Middle East, people began to rear pigs, sheep and cows for food, milk and fleeces, and sewed fields with wheat and barley. Growing crops and raising animals meant that people didn't have to travel far and wide to hunt and forage for food. Groups could settle in one place and form communities. However, farmers had to endure hours of back-breaking work to grow their precious crops, which limited how much food they could produce.

TRACTOR VERSUS HORSE

Ever since farming began, humans have turned to animals for help – reared to be strong and obedient, oxen, horses and mules proved perfect for pulling ploughs and wagons. In the 1920s, there were 25 million horses and mules being used on American farms alone. However, working farm animals needed to be housed, fed and looked after – which was expensive and time-consuming – and if they fell ill their work couldn't be completed. The invention of the petrol-driven tractor in the early 1900s changed everything. After years of development and improvements, more and more farmers replaced their faithful, hard-working animals for the convenience and power of the tractor.

THE FIRST FARM MACHINES

The first movable farm vehicle was the steam-powered traction engine. These heavy machines worked like steam engines – with a boiler, chimney and firebox – and could travel on roads. Some farms used them to haul loads, plough fields or provide power to other machines like threshers and saws. Traction engines were used in the second half of the 19th century but were too expensive and cumbersome to be truly successful.

THE N-SERIES 8N

The invention of the internal combustion engine sparked a rush to create a light yet powerful tractor that could do the work of a whole team of horses. In 1938, the Ford Motor Company (see page 36) partnered with tractor designer Harry Ferguson to produce one of the most successful tractors of all time: the N-series. This little tractor was strong enough to haul any farm implement, yet so lightweight it could climb slopes and trundle along slippery tracks; it had an incredibly reliable engine and a new type of trailer hitch that made ploughing more effective. It was also relatively cheap. Farmers all over the world loved it, and in some places use them even to this day.

HOW THE TRACTOR CHANGED THE WORLD

The introduction of the Ford N-series marks the time when petrol-driven tractors became useful and cheap enough for farmers to use instead of working farm animals. Cheap to run, easy to maintain and capable of working non-stop, the N-series made life much easier. Nowadays, tractors are used for a huge variety of jobs, including harrowing (breaking up soil) and ploughing fields, sowing seeds, spreading fertilizer, reaping crops and pulling trailers. Without tractors, there's no way that farmers would be able to grow the huge harvests needed to feed our world's growing population.

FIGHTER PLANES
WARRIORS OF THE SKY

Made from wood, canvas and wire, the first fighter planes appeared over the muddy battlefields of the First World War. Pilots in open cockpits observed enemy positions and duelled each other in whirling, nerve-shredding dogfights. By the Second World War, fighter planes were faster, stronger and more manoeuvrable. When pilots throttled up their aircrafts they smelled the acrid exhaust fumes, felt the engine's vibration and every bump on the runway – and then the smooth, graceful climb into the sky.

FACTS AND STATS

- » AIRCRAFT NAME: Spitfire
- » MANUFACTURED BY: Supermarine, UK
- » PRIMARY USER: Royal Air Force
- » SERVICE LIFE: 1938–1948
- » NUMBER BUILT: 20,300+
- » CREW: 1
- » POWERED BY: Liquid-cooled Rolls Royce Merlin V12 piston engine
- » ENGINE POWER: 2,050 hp
- » TOP SPEED: 710 kph
- » MAX ALTITUDE: 11,100 m
- » RANGE: 770 km
- » ARMAMENT: Machine guns and cannons
- » DIMENSIONS: Length: 9.12 m; Wingspan: 11.23 m; Height: 3.48 m

FACTS AND STATS

- » AIRCRAFT NAME: P-51 Mustang
- » MANUFACTURED BY: North American Aviation, USA
- » PRIMARY USER: United States Army Air Force (USAAF)
- » SERVICE LIFE: 1942–1953
- » NUMBER BUILT: 15,000+
- » CREW: 1
- » POWERED BY: Liquid-cooled Packard/Rolls Royce Merlin V12 piston engine
- » ENGINE POWER: 1,490 hp
- » TOP SPEED: 708 kph
- » MAX ALTITUDE: 12,800 m
- » RANGE: 2,656 km
- » ARMAMENT: Machine guns
- » DIMENSIONS: Length: 9.8 m; Wingspan: 11.3 m; Height: 4 m

» AIRCRAFT NAME: Bf 109
» MANUFACTURED BY: Messerschmitt AG, Germany
» PRIMARY USER: Luftwaffe (German Air Force)
» SERVICE LIFE: 1937–1945
» NUMBER BUILT: 33,984
» CREW: 1
» POWERED BY: Liquid-cooled Daimler-Benz DB 605A-1 V12 piston engine
» ENGINE POWER: 1,455 hp
» TOP SPEED: 588 kph
» MAX ALTITUDE: 12,000 m
» RANGE: 600 km
» ARMAMENT: Machine guns and cannons
» DIMENSIONS: Length: 9 m; Wingspan: 10 m; Height: 2.6 m

FACTS AND STATS

» AIRCRAFT NAME: A6M 'Zero'
» MANUFACTURED BY: Mitsubishi Heavy Industries, Japan
» PRIMARY USER: Imperial Japanese Navy Air Service
» SERVICE LIFE: 1940–1945
» NUMBER BUILT: 10,000+
» CREW: 1
» POWERED BY: Air-cooled Nakajima NK1C Sakae-12 14-cylinder piston engine
» ENGINE POWER: 1,130 hp
» TOP SPEED: 565 kph
» MAX ALTITUDE: 11,000 m
» RANGE: 1,870 km
» ARMAMENT: Machine guns and cannons
» DIMENSIONS: Length: 9 m; Wingspan: 12 m; Height: 3 m

HOW THE FIGHTER PLANE CHANGED THE WORLD

Fighter planes have changed a lot since their introduction a century ago: metal has replaced wood and canvas; jets have replaced piston engines; sophisticated electronics have replaced purely manual controls; and missiles have replaced machine guns. Some can be launched from aircraft carriers, others like the Lockheed F35 Lightning can even hover in the air like helicopters. Nowadays, nearly every country in the world uses fighter planes to carry out reconnaissance duties and protect themselves and their allies from attack.

STEEL BATTLESHIP
FLOATING FORTRESSES

In April 1945, towards the end of the Second World War, the largest, heaviest and most powerful battleship ever constructed set out on her final voyage. The pride of the Japanese fleet and built at huge cost to rule the waves, *Yamato* was a true giant of the ocean – sailors said she hardly pitched or rolled even in rough seas. And yet, like all battleships, she was vulnerable to air attack and after a desperate battle against hundreds of American bombers, she sank into the Pacific taking most of her crew with her.

FACTS AND STATS

» **CLASS:** Yamato
» **VESSEL NAME:** *Yamato* (which means 'Great Harmony')
» **BUILT BY:** Imperial Japanese Navy
» **LAUNCHED:** 8 August 1940
» **SUNK:** 7 April 1945
» **NUMBER OF CLASS BUILT:** 3 (of a planned 5)
» **CREW:** 2,700
» **POWERED BY:** 150,000 shp engine
» **TOP SPEED:** 50 kph
» **RANGE:** 13,300 km
» **AIRCRAFT:** 7 Nakajima E8N seaplanes
» **DIMENSIONS:** Length: 263 m; Width (or 'Beam'): 38.9 m; Displacement: 71,659 long tonnes; Draught: 11 m

AIRCRAFT

Up to seven Nakajima E8N seaplanes could be stored in the hangers inside *Yamato*'s stern. After being launched from one of two 18-metre catapults, the E8Ns flew around looking out for enemy vessels or incoming aircraft. The aircraft's three floats allowed them to land alongside the ship, where cranes picked them up and put them back in their hangers.

ANTI-AIRCRAFT GUNS

Yamato's designers knew that despite her huge size and thick armour, their ship could be sunk by bombs and torpedoes dropped by aeroplanes. To prevent enemy aircraft getting too close, they added 168 anti-aircraft guns to be manned by the sailors.

MAIN ARMAMENT

Yamato's nine biggest guns were placed in three turrets, which moved left and right to aim at targets. At 21 metres long, 46 centimentres wide, and each weighing 147 tonnes, they were the largest guns ever fitted to a battleship. Each turret could hurl shells weighing 1,460 kilograms up to 42 kilometres, which is like firing a car from Dover, UK to Calais, France. Sailors had to stand 10 metres away from the guns when they fired to avoid suffering severe burns.

SUPERSTRUCTURE

The parts of the ship (except the gun turrets) that rise above the deck are called the 'superstructure'. This is where the navigation and radar detection equipment are kept. Near the top is the bridge, from where the vessel was steered and the captain gave his commands. Lookouts with searchlights and binoculars kept watch for ships, submarines and enemy aircraft.

ENGINES AND PROPELLERS

Yamato was fast for such a huge ship. Twelve oil-fired boilers transformed water into super-heated steam, which turned four turbines. These steam-powered turbines rotated the ship's four propellers, giving her a top speed of 50 kilometres per hour. However, this used up a lot of oil, limiting how far *Yamato* could travel without a refill.

BELOW DECKS

Inside the ship were endless corridors lined with hissing pipes and bundles of electric cables; hundreds of watertight doors; fuel tanks for the throbbing engines; ammunition stores; workshops and piles of spare parts; crew quarters; larders; kitchens and dining rooms; and toilets and showers. The crew had to work hard, be prepared for action at all times, and were dealt harsh punishments if they failed in their duties.

HOW THE STEEL BATTLESHIP CHANGED THE WORLD

From the late 19th to the early 20th centuries, battleships were the most feared warships on the sea. Covered in thick armour, they were designed to carry guns powerful enough to bombard coastlines and sink any vessel from many kilometres away. These gigantic steel behemoths were expensive to design, build and maintain, and so became a way for countries to show their rivals how rich, powerful and dangerous they were.

KON-TIKI RAFT
IMPOSSIBLE VOYAGE

Imagine being on a wooden raft with no sides or engine in the middle of the Pacific Ocean. You cannot steer, so you're gambling that the ocean currents will take you all the way from Peru to Polynesia. There's not a scrap of land within 2,000 kilometres; the deep blue sea and boundless sky seem to stretch on forever, and yet you're not alone because sharks glide beneath the deck, waiting patiently for their next meal. This might sound far-fetched, but in 1947, six adventurers made a voyage just like this on a raft called *Kon-Tiki*.

FACTS AND STATS

- » **VESSEL NAME:** *Kon-Tiki*
- » **VESSEL TYPE:** Balsa wood raft
- » **CREW:** 6
- » **VOYAGE:** 6,900 km from Peru to Polynesia
- » **VOYAGE LENGTH:** 101 days (28 April–7 August 1947)
- » **POWERED BY:** Wind, ocean currents and paddles
- » **AVERAGE SPEED:** 68 km per day
- » **DIMENSIONS:** Length: 5.5 m; Width: 3.7 m; Sail height: 5.5 m; Sail width: 4.6 m

JOURNEY WITH A PURPOSE

Thor Heyerdahl was a Norwegian zoologist and adventurer. He believed that Polynesia – a group of over 1,000 islands spread across the South Pacific Ocean – was settled in around 500 AD by explorers from South America, and not (as is generally accepted today) by navigators from South Asia (see Polynesian Canoe, page 6). Thor decided to prove that people from Peru could have sailed across the Pacific to Polynesia by building his own balsa wood raft and making the crossing himself – even though he had never sailed a boat before and couldn't even swim.

A GALLANT CREW

Thor could not sail 6,900 kilometres alone – he needed a brave crew to help him. Herman Watzinger was an engineer who helped Thor design *Kon-Tiki*; Bengt Danielsson was in charge of food and supplies; Erik Hesselberg was the only sailor and navigator among the crew; Torstein Raaby and Knut Haugland operated the radios, and Lorita was a South American parrot who kept the crew company and spoke Spanish.

AN ANCIENT CRAFT

Thor made his raft using only the designs, methods and natural materials that were available to the ancient Peruvians 1,500 years ago. The flat part of the raft (the 'float') was made from huge balsa wood tree trunks, lashed together with hemp rope. The bow was made from planks of pine, formed into a 'V' shape to help it cut through the water. The mast was formed from mango wood and held a canvas sail. The deck was made from split bamboo and bamboo matting. The cabin had bamboo plait walls and a banana leaf roof.

HOW THE *KON-TIKI* CHANGED THE WORLD

The world celebrated when Thor and his intrepid crew finished their amazing voyage. Thor proved his belief that it would have been possible for the ancient people of Peru to ride the winds and ocean currents on their amazing rafts all the way to the South Pacific. Although he admitted that this alone didn't prove that was what actually happened, he challenged the world to at least consider his theory.

PROVISIONS

The crew took a mixture of food that the ancient Polynesians would have had, such as coconuts (Lorita's favourite), sweet potatoes, nuts and fruit, as well as dried and tinned food provided by the US Army. One thousand litres of water was stored in cans and sealed bamboo rods. They also caught lots of flying fish, tuna and shark to eat.

AN EPIC JOURNEY

Thor relied on wind and ocean currents to carry him westward across the Pacific. The crew had many adventures on their 101-day voyage, including close encounters with sharks and enormous whale sharks, a three-day gale that split their sail, and a man overboard who had to be rescued. The journey ended when the raft crashed onto a shallow reef in Polynesia.

DEEP-SEA SUBMERSIBLE
INTO THE ABYSS

In January 1960, two explorers began an epic voyage straight down into the lightless depths of the Pacific Ocean. They watched as strange creatures drifted past the porthole, lit up by the submersible's lamps. The abyss beneath them was kilometres deep; their destination the seabed. Down they went, deeper and deeper, as the metal that separated them from instant death creaked, groaned and strained under the intense and ever-growing pressure.

DESIGNED FOR THE DEPTHS

The *Trieste* is a submersible – a vehicle built to travel underwater – and was designed by Swiss inventor and explorer Auguste Piccard. He called it a 'bathyscaphe', which means 'deep ship'. Its task was to explore far, far deeper than any normal submarine could go, using its own ballast and buoyancy tanks to control its vertical dives and ascents.

FUEL UP

In the 1930s, Auguste Piccard designed a spherical air-tight gondola attached to a helium-filled balloon, which he used to reach a record-breaking altitude of 23 kilometres. When Auguste turned his inventive mind from the sky to the sea, he used the same principles of balloon flight for the *Trieste*. The cylindrical portion of the *Trieste* (the 'float') acts like a balloon, but instead of lighter-than-air helium, it's filled with lighter-than-water petrol.

DEEPEST DIVE

In January 1960, US naval officer Don Walsh and engineer Jacques Piccard (Auguste's son) descended 10,916 metres to the deepest place on Earth: the Challenger Deep. If Mount Everest was placed there, its peak would still be two kilometres underwater. The trip down took four hours and 48 minutes, "travelling about the speed of an elderly elevator," as Piccard described. It was the first time any vessel had reached such a depth. The total journey took just under nine hours, with the two men sitting inside the cold, cramped gondola.

FACTS AND STATS

» **VESSEL NAME:** *Trieste*
» **VESSEL TYPE:** Bathyscaphe
» **DESIGNED BY:** Auguste and Jacques Piccard
» **SERVICE LIFE:** 1953–1966
» **CREW:** 2
» **POWERED BY:** 2 x 2 hp electric motors driving propellers
» **TOP HORIZONTAL SPEED:** 2 kph
» **DEEPEST DIVE:** 10,916 m
» **DIMENSIONS:** Length: 18 m; Width (or 'Beam'): 3.5 m; Displacement: 50 long tonnes; Gondola width: 2.16 m

A BALLOON THAT SINKS

To dive, the *Trieste* needed enough ballast on board to outweigh the lighter-than-water petrol in the 11 buoyancy tanks, and become heavier than water. Nine tonnes of iron pellets were stored inside two containers – enough to cause the *Trieste* to descend into the sea. When the pilots wanted to return to the surface, they opened the containers and allowed the iron pellets to tumble out.

HOW THE *TRIESTE* CHANGED THE WORLD

The *Trieste*'s record-breaking plunge into the Challenger Deep proved that creatures had adapted to exist even at the most extreme depths of the ocean. This triggered a tidal wave of interest in underwater exploration, marine biology and oceanography. It also proved that the bathyscaphe could reach anywhere beneath the world's oceans, and the technology invented by the Piccards was used to build later research bathyscaphes.

UNDER PRESSURE

One of the biggest problems for submersibles is surviving the outside pressure – the weight of all that water above bearing down on them. If they're not strong enough, they'll implode like an egg crushed in a fist. The *Trieste*'s 'float' was safe because the petrol inside equalised the outside water pressure without any problems – but the gondola crew compartment was another story. It was designed as a sphere because that is the most pressure-resistant shape, had 13-centimetre-thick steel walls, contained a single, cone-shaped window made from Plexiglass, and could withstand pressures of up to around one tonne per square centimetre.

HELICOPTER
CHOPPERS AND WHIRLYBIRDS

The Bell 'Huey' is one of the most successful and adaptable helicopters ever produced. First built in 1959, these rugged, multi-purpose vehicles were made in their thousands and are still used all over the world today. Pilots love flying these powerful workhorses of the sky, with one describing his first experience of taking off in a Huey like this: "The machine left the ground like it was falling up."

FACTS AND STATS

» **PICTURED MODEL NAME:** Bell UH-1H 'Huey'
» **BUILT BY:** Bell Helicopter, USA
» **ENTERED SERVICE:** 1959 (Bell UH-1 – first model); 1966 (Bell UH-1H – later model, pictured)
» **NUMBER BUILT:** 16,000+
» **CREW:** 1 or 2 pilots
» **PASSENGERS:** 13
» **POWERED BY:** 1400 hp Lycoming T53-L-13
» **TOP SPEED:** 217 kph
» **RANGE:** 507 km
» **DIMENSIONS:** Length: 17.3 m; Width: 2.6 m; Height: 4.2 m; Rotor diameter: 14.6 m

VTOL

Helicopters are Vertical Take-Off and Landing (VTOL) vehicles, meaning they take off straight up (vertically) into the air and land the same way. The huge amount of vertical lift this requires is created by the horizontal rotor blades located on top; the faster they spin the more lift they create, until the helicopter takes off.

FLYING FIREFIGHTERS

This is one of nine helicopters operated by Cal Fire – the Department of Forestry and Fire Protection in the American state of California. As soon as a forest fire is reported, these specially modified Hueys can take off and reach even the most remote sites quickly to drop off firefighter crews and soak the flames with water. Water is dumped either from a bucket towed on a cable or a tank suspended underneath the cabin; these can be refilled from nearby lakes.

EYES IN THE SKY

Helicopters can travel quickly, slowly, or hover in one place for as long as they like; they are nimble, can fly at high and low altitudes, and be kitted out with cameras, searchlights, heat-detecting equipment and loudspeaker systems. All this makes helicopters perfect for use by police forces and news companies: they can follow speeding cars and fleeing suspects; hover over crime scenes, disasters and accident sites, and sporting or public events; and record and report what they see to people on the ground.

PASSENGER TRANSPORT

Helicopters are ideal for transporting small numbers of passengers to remote places where aeroplanes can't land, such as oil rigs, ships, Arctic or mountain research stations and the tops of buildings. And even if it cannot touch down (in dense jungle, for example), people and cargo can be winched on and off as the helicopter hovers above.

LIFESAVERS

Helicopters are the ideal vehicle to carry out search and rescue operations, looking for people who are lost or injured in the wilderness. Once located, the people can be lifted straight up into the hovering helicopter using a winch and pulley system, and flown to the nearest hospital. Helicopters can also be modified to become air ambulances by fitting out the cabin with emergency medical equipment and space for wheeled stretchers ('gurneys').

HOW THE HELICOPTER CHANGED THE WORLD

Fast, agile and able to land pretty much anywhere, helicopters like the Bell Huey changed the world – not only by transporting passengers and cargo, but also by becoming an emergency response vehicle. If you were lost at sea, trapped on a mountain or caught in a wildfire, what better sound could there be than the steady *whup-whup-whup* of an approaching helicopter.

SNOWMOBILE
SWIFT SNOW FLOATER

In the 1950s, a Canadian inventor called Joseph-Armand Bombardier declared that one day he would: "invent a little machine that will float on snow." His dream was to create a vehicle that could travel quickly and safely over ice and snow without the need for a trained dog team. After many years of experimentation, he succeeded in designing the snowmobile – a light machine propelled by a single caterpillar track and steered with a pair of skis.

EARLY DESIGNS

Motorised vehicles that could travel over snow were being designed in the early 1900s, not long after the invention of the combustion engine. Cars like the famous Ford Model T (see page 36) could be converted into 'snowflyers' by replacing their wheels with caterpillar tracks and skis, although these were too heavy to be completely successful. It was Joseph-Armand Bombardier who eventually came up with the lightweight snowmobile design we all recognise today.

FACTS AND STATS

» **SNOWMOBILE NAME:** K60 Ski-Doo
» **BUILDER:** Bombardier Inc, Canada
» **YEAR PRODUCTION BEGAN:** 1960
» **POWERED BY:** 7 hp 4-stroke Kohler petrol engine
» **TOP SPEED:** 30 kph (approx.)
» **DIMENSIONS:** Length: 277 cm; Width: 79 cm; Height: 76 cm; Weight: 152 kg

ONE TRACK, TWO SKIS

Snowmobiles are designed to travel over snow and ice. A single caterpillar track grips the snowy surface and drives the vehicle forward; this track is nearly as wide as the snowmobile itself and is driven by a petrol engine located at the front. To guide the vehicle through the snow, the driver uses handlebars to turn a pair of front-mounted skis. Spring suspension and a comfortable seat make riding across hard or uneven snow smoother.

A HAPPY ACCIDENT

Joseph-Armand Bombardier originally wanted to call his new invention the 'Ski-Dog' because it had skis and was designed to replace sledge dogs. However, the name was misspelled in the advertising brochures as the 'Ski-Doo'. Luckily, Bombardier thought the name Ski-Doo worked really well and decided to keep it.

STUNT-MOBILES

Modern snowmobiles are much more powerful than Bombardier's original designs. Nowadays, most snowmobile engines are between 100 and 180 horsepower, reach top speeds of over 150 kilometres per hour, can travel over really rough terrain, and perform impressive stunts and jumps.

SAFETY IN THE SNOW

Nowadays, drivers are attached to their snowmobiles with a safety cord. The safety cord is pulled out of the vehicle if they fall off. This shuts down the engine and stops the snowmobile from speeding away without anyone being in control.

HOW THE SNOWMOBILE CHANGED THE WORLD

The snowmobile changed the lives of people living in isolated, snowbound communities like those found in North America, Canada and Scandinavia. Before, people relied on snowshoes and sledges pulled by dog teams to hunt, travel and collect supplies. Unlike snowshoes, snowmobiles are faster and take less effort to use; unlike dogs, snowmobiles start at the press of a button, are easier to drive, and cheaper to maintain. These powerful, lightweight machines have made life safer, easier and more fun for those who live in the most hostile environments on Earth.

DIESEL LOCOMOTIVE
WORKHORSES OF THE RAILWAYS

When a driver presses the start button on a Class 55 Deltic diesel locomotive, it sounds like a thousand stones being rattled inside a giant tin drum. This is quickly followed by a mighty roar, a blast of hot exhaust smoke and a deep throaty rumble. Since the 1960s, the railways of Britain – and all over the world – have been dominated by powerful machines like this, hauling cargo and carriages safely and swiftly over gleaming steel tracks.

FACTS AND STATS

» **CLASS:** British Rail Class 55 Deltic
» **LOCOMOTIVE NAME:** D9009 *Alycidon*
» **BUILT BY:** English Electric, UK
» **SERVICE LIFE:** 1961–1980
» **NUMBER BUILT:** 22
» **CREW:** 1
» **POWERED BY:** 2 x 18-cylinder Napier Deltic diesel engines
» **ENGINE POWER:** 1650 hp per engine
» **TOP SPEED:** 161 kph
» **DIMENSIONS:** Length: 21 m; Width: 2.68 m; Height: 3.9 m; Weight: 100 tonnes

THE MIGHTY DELTIC

The Deltic was the first diesel passenger express locomotive in Britain capable of travelling at 160 kilometres per hour for long distances. Its two engines were designed for Royal Navy patrol boats before being adapted for use in locomotives.

DIESEL DEVELOPMENT

The diesel engine was invented by a German mechanical engineer called Rudolph Diesel in 1892. By the early 1900s they were being used to power experimental trains. At first, diesel engines were too heavy and underpowered to be successful, but over time many improvements were made. From the 1930s onward, locomotives powered by diesel engines were being used more and more to haul passenger and freight trains.

1N03

THE WEST RIDING

DRIVING THE DELTIC

Driving the Deltic was a very different experience to driving a steam locomotive – it was still a highly skilled job but far less physically demanding. There was no more heaving coal into a red-hot firebox, and no more open cabs exposed to the wind and rain. The driver sat in a comfortable, upholstered chair, controlling the engine using buttons, brake handles and a throttle lever. There was a hotplate to brew up tea, and a washbasin and toilet inside the train's nose.

HOW THE DIESEL LOCOMOTIVE CHANGED THE WORLD

Diesel locomotives transformed railways all over the world by replacing the steam engine. They are faster, more reliable, easier to operate, can haul heavier loads and can travel further without refuelling. They also require less maintenance, create less smoke and pollution, and don't produce sparks and cinders that can cause fires. These diesel-driven workhorses still lead the way in hauling freight, although it's likely that more environmentally friendly electric locomotives will begin to take over in the future.

D9009

BRITISH RAILWAYS

TRACTION CONTROL

Sometimes diesel locomotives lose grip (or 'traction') on the rails, and their wheels start to spin. This can be caused by icy conditions or when hauling a heavy load up a hill. To deal with this, many diesel trains have a device called a 'sander' fitted by their front wheels. If the driver feels the train slipping or losing traction they turn on the sander, which uses jets of air to blow sand onto the rails. This increases the wheels' grip and the train can continue on its way.

DIESEL POWER

Diesel fuel is used for the heavy job of hauling freight because it's cheaper and more efficient than petrol, produces less carbon dioxide (which contributes to global warming) and is less likely to catch fire or explode. However, it still creates harmful emissions that pollute the atmosphere and are bad for your health when breathed in.

HOW DIESELS HAUL

Electric locomotives draw the power they need to move either from overhead electric cables or a third rail on the ground. Diesel locomotives are different – they create their own electricity. The rumbling engine generates electricity, which is transferred to smaller electric traction motors near each of the two six-wheel bogies. It's these motors that drive the wheels. So, in fact, these vehicles should be called diesel-electric locomotives.

AUTO RICKSHAW
MINI MACHINES

Often brightly coloured and beeping their horns, auto rickshaws are found in cities all over the world, and especially in India, Africa, the Middle East and Southeast Asia. Streets swarm with these puttering, spluttering little vehicles, which can zip in, out and around the flow of traffic to pick up passengers, make deliveries and get from place to place as quickly as possible.

FACTS AND STATS

» **OTHER NAMES:** Bajaj, Chand Gari, Tuk-tuk

» **PASSENGERS:** 4
(1 driver, 3 passengers)

» **POWERED BY:** 2- or 4-stroke single cylinder engine

» **FUELLED BY:** Various, including petrol, diesel and compressed natural gas (CNG)

» **ENGINE POWER:** 7 hp (approx.)

» **TOP SPEED:** 80 kph

» **AVERAGE SPEED:** 50–60 kph

» **GEARS:** 4 forward, 1 reverse

» **DIMENSIONS:** Length: 2.62 m; Width: 1.3 m; Height: 1.7 m; Weight: 610 kg

RICKSHAWS

Auto rickshaws are more modern, motorised versions of a much older vehicle called a 'rickshaw'. Rickshaws were first used in the late 1800s in Japan ('rickshaw' comes from a Japanese word that means 'human-powered vehicle'). They were small wooden carriages just big enough for one passenger to sit in, and which ran on two wide-spoked wheels. It was pulled along by a driver who gripped two long bars extending from the vehicle's front.

VERSATILE VEHICLE

Auto rickshaws are good to use in hot places because their open sides mean the driver and passengers can enjoy a breeze as they zoom along. They are also a practical alternative to the car: they are cheaper to buy, easier to maintain because of their simple design, and don't use up as much fuel. Although best suited to busy town and city streets, auto rickshaws can be used in the countryside and the open road, although their small engines do struggle to climb hills.

HOW THE AUTO RICKSHAW CHANGED THE WORLD

Affordable, easy to maintain and perfect for zipping along busy roads, the auto rickshaw has transformed people's lives, especially those in developing countries. The auto rickshaw provides people who cannot afford a car a vehicle they can use as personal transport, or a way to earn money as a taxi service or delivery driver. They are also seen as a way to reduce the number of larger vehicles on the roads (such as cars and vans), which produce more of the harmful air pollution that causes illness.

DUCKING AND DRIVING

Driving an auto rickshaw is like being in control of a cross between a motorbike and a small car. Although a roof and windscreen keep the driver and passengers partially protected, the lack of side doors leaves them exposed to outside noise, heat or cold, and traffic fumes. It takes skill to weave an auto rickshaw in and out of traffic on busy city streets because although they don't travel very quickly, the single front wheel means they can tip over if the driver takes a corner too tightly.

CABLE CAR
FOR PLACES HIGH AND HARD TO REACH

Medellín is the second largest city in the South American country of Colombia – a busy, vibrant place with a rich cultural history and a population of two and a half million. Its modern Metro train system is the city's pride and joy, transporting 500,000 passengers to and from work every day. However, some areas of Medellín are far too hilly for trains and even buses to get to, leaving the people who live there virtually stranded. So, in 2004, a brand-new form of mass public transport was introduced to reach them: the Metrocable.

THE PYLONS

Pylons (or 'towers') are placed along the route to support the cable and the cars above the ground, and guide them to and from the stations; the cable car's grips are fixed to the top of the cable, which allows them to 'ride' over a set of wheels on the pylon.

FACTS AND STATS

- » CABLE CAR TYPE: Gondola lift
- » OPERATED BY: Medellín Metro, Colombia
- » OPENED: 2004
- » NUMBER OF STATIONS: 15
- » SYSTEM LENGTH: 14.6 km
- » CREW: 0
- » PASSENGERS PER YEAR: 16 million
- » AVERAGE SPEED: 18 kph
- » DIMENSIONS: Length: 1.8 m; Width: 2 m; Height: 2.3 m

THE CABLE

Each Metrocable line uses a single steel cable formed into a loop. These cables are made from lots of thin steel strands, twisted together like rope, which makes them flexible and very strong. Each car is fixed to the cable by a 'grip', and as the cable moves it carries the car along with it.

THE STATION

This is where passengers get on and off the cable car. It's also where the electric motor is located that moves the cable and the attached cars. At each end of the line is a large, horizontal wheel that supports the cable and helps it move smoothly; as cable cars go round these wheels, they change direction from going up the line to going back down for their return journey.

FROM INDUSTRY TO TOURISM

Cable cars have been in use for about 200 years. They were first used to transport goods grown or dug out from high up in hills and mountains – such as timber, tea leaves, coffee beans, coal and ore – to the bottom, usually in large metal buckets. From the early 1900s, cable cars were also built to give sightseeing tourists and holidaymakers spectacular views over natural beauty spots. Nowadays they are mostly used in ski resorts, quickly transporting skiers to the top of the snowy slopes.

THE CAR

Metrocable passengers take a seat on metal benches and gaze through large windows as the mountainous slopes, trees, shops, cafes and winding streets of Medellín pass gently by below. At the end of their short and relaxing journey they can transfer to the Metro train or head out on foot. The Metrocable system puts everything the city centre has to offer within easy reach of even the poorest citizens.

HOW THE CABLE CAR CHANGED THE WORLD

The Metrocable has made a huge difference to the lives of people in Medellín. Before, people living in the hilly outskirts had to walk for two and a half hours to reach the city centre. Now, the cable car system makes the same journey in a mere 20 minutes, putting jobs, education and healthcare within easy and affordable reach. Systems similar to the Metrocable are now working in other countries too, including Singapore, Turkey, Mexico, Bolivia, Brazil and Venezuela, bringing people there the same advantages and opportunities.

HIGH-SPEED TRAIN
FAST AS A BULLET

In 1964, a remarkable new machine began racing between the Japanese cities of Tokyo and Ōsaka. The 0 Series Shinkansen high-speed train, with its blue-and-white livery and nose like a bullet, looks modern – futuristic, even – despite being over 50 years old. The world was immediately enthralled when these sleek and elegant racehorses on rails first appeared – no one had ever seen anything like them before – and soon other countries were rushing to build their own.

FACTS AND STATS

» **TRAIN TYPE:** High Speed Train (HST)
» **CLASS:** 0 Series
» **OPERATED BY:** JNR (Japanese National Railways)
» **SERVICE LIFE:** 1964–2008
» **NUMBER BUILT:** 3,216
» **CREW:** 1 driver
» **PASSENGERS:** 1,340 (on a 16-carriage train)
» **TOP SPEED:** 210 kph (1964–1985); 220 kph (1986–2008)
» **DIMENSIONS (PER CAR):** Length: 25 m; Width: 3.3 m; Height: 4.2 m

PLANES, TRAINS AND AUTOMOBILES

By the 1950s, trains were considered a slow and old-fashioned way to get about, especially when compared to the convenience of owning your own automobile (see page 36) and the speed of commercial jet airliners (see page 86). But the Japanese government decided to build a new railway – and their creation would be far faster and more reliable than anything that had gone before. They named it the 'Shinkansen', which means 'New Main Line', but the iconic design and the way it seemed to fly over the rails soon earned it the nickname 'Bullet Train'.

NEW TRACKS, NEW TRAINS

The first Shinkansen line (between Tokyo and Ōsaka) needed new rails and trains. Five hundred kilometres of track was laid in as straight a line as possible to ensure the trains could run at maximum speed; 113 kilometres of tunnel was blasted out of solid rock; 3,000 new bridges were built, and there were to be no level crossings – all roads had to go over or under the track. All of this, as well as designing and building the 0 Series, was achieved in only five years.

REGULAR AND RELIABLE

In its first three years, the Shinkansen delivered 100 million passengers; by 1976 that grew to one billion. To this day, a total of 10 billion journeys have been made on the Shinkansen. At peak times trains leave Tokyo station every three minutes; they're rarely late, and even when they are it's usually only by a few seconds. Amazingly, over the Shinkansen's decades-long history, there has not been a single passenger death due to accidents or derailments.

A SPEEDY SUCCESS

The 0 Series trains reached speeds of 210 kilometres per hour – about twice as fast as any other train in the world at that time – cutting the journey time between Tokyo and Ōsaka from six and a half hours to only three. This drew the cities closer together – people could hop on a train to visit friends, family, go shopping, or attend business meetings, and be back home in time for supper.

HOW THE SHINKANSEN CHANGED THE WORLD

The Shinkansen 0 Series introduced a new and exciting age of high-speed railways. It's estimated that the reduced journey times has saved the Japanese 400 million hours of time and £3.7 billion per year. The world has benefited too – after seeing the Shinkansen's safe, reliable and lightning-fast service, other countries built their own high-speed railway lines for sleek and speedy trains to glide effortlessly over.

SPY PLANE
SPEED, STEALTH AND SURVEILLANCE

The SR-71 Blackbird's fuselage looks like a spear tip; its razor-sharp edges and wide, flattened underside gives it the resemblance of a manta ray – it certainly cuts through the air as easily as any fish does through water – and those two fire-breathing engines come shrieking straight from a scene in a science fiction film. It's true that this miracle of engineering looks as if it's travelled to us from the future, and yet it first took to the air over half a century ago.

FACTS AND STATS

- » **AIRCRAFT NAME:** SR-71 Blackbird
- » **OTHER NAMES:** Sled, Habu and Lady in Black
- » **MANUFACTURED BY:** Lockheed, USA
- » **BUILT FOR:** US Air Force and National Aeronautics and Space Administration (NASA), USA
- » **SERVICE LIFE:** 1966–1999
- » **NUMBER BUILT:** 32
- » **CREW:** 2 (pilot and reconnaissance systems officer (RSO))
- » **POWERED BY:** 2 x Pratt & Whitney J58 afterburning turbojets
- » **TOP SPEED:** 3,540 kph / Mach 3.32 (approx.)
- » **MAX ALTITUDE:** 25,908 m
- » **CLIMB RATE:** 3,603 mpm
- » **RANGE:** 5,926 km
- » **DIMENSIONS:** Length: 32.74 m; Wingspan: 16.94 m; Height: 5.64 m

TOP SECRET

The Cold War (1947–1991) was a time of great distrust between the Western countries headed by the USA, and the Eastern countries headed by the USSR (now called Russia). Each side wanted to discover the other's secrets and used 'spy planes' to take photographs of enemy territory from the sky. In the late 1950s, US president Lyndon Johnson ordered a new aircraft to be designed that could never be shot down. So, the SR-71 was hatched in Lockheed's Skunk Works research facility in California.

SPIES IN THE SKY

The SR-71's job was to take photographs of enemy territory (the locations of nuclear missile facilities, for example) and carry them back to base for analysis. Different types of spy equipment such as cameras and imaging radars could be fitted to the Blackbird inside removable nosecones. The Blackbird could photograph 160,934 square kilometres of land per hour, and used a film roll that was around three kilometres long. The photographs were so good, it was possible to identify objects on the ground that were smaller than a shoe.

INVISIBLE AND INVINCIBLE

Blackbird was one of the first stealth planes. Its narrow shape, sharp 'chines' (the blade-like edges on the fuselage), the way the fuselage blended into the wings, and the black paint that cooled its surface temperature meant it was difficult to detect on radar. Over 1,000 surface-to-air missiles (SAMs) were fired at Blackbirds, and not a single one hit. All the Blackbird pilot had to do was increase speed, and by the time the missile reached the right spot he was long gone.

HOW THE SR-71 BLACKBIRD CHANGED THE WORLD

Some vehicles are marvels of technology, others are icons of style – the SR-71 is both. The design and look of modern stealth aircraft such as the F117 Nighthawk and the F35 Lightning can be traced back 60 years to the Blackbird's invention and its 30 years of successful service. As well as playing an important role during the Cold War, it also holds many world records including the highest (25,929 metres) and fastest (3,530 kilometres per hour) manned aircraft.

BLACKBIRD MISSIONS

Blackbirds could only perform one mission per week because of all the planning and preparation that was needed. Before take-off, the pilot and RSO (who operated the spy equipment) ate a high-energy meal of steak and eggs. During flight, food (including macaroni cheese, beef with gravy, and butterscotch pudding) and drink (water, iced tea or fruit juices) were sucked from tubes, which could be warmed up by holding them against the window.

EXPERT CREW

Operating the Blackbird required complete and utter concentration from the pilot and RSO – any mistake could lead to disaster not just for them, but for the whole world. Only the very best aviators were selected to fly the Blackbird, and they underwent the same rigorous training as NASA astronauts; Neil Armstrong, the first man on the Moon (see Saturn V, page 88), was a Blackbird test pilot before he joined the space program.

FORMULA ONE RACING CAR
SPEED MACHINES

The Lotus 49 first lined up on the starting grid at the 1967 Dutch Grand Prix. Spectators watched enthralled as the air filled with exhaust fumes and the deafening roar of revving engines – and then, in a haze of tyre smoke, they were off, 17 bunched-up racing cars swerving and sliding around each other in a battle to reach the front. Lotus 49 number '5' was two-time world champion Jim Clark's car, and he went on to win even though it was the first time he'd driven it.

FAST FORMULA

The Formula One World Championship is the fastest motorsport in the world. For 70 years expert drivers have raced cars, designed using cutting-edge technology, for the glory of becoming champion. Races (called Grand Prix, which means 'grand prize') are held on specially built tracks – although some circuits, such as Monaco, are created by closing off public streets. The prizes are fame, glory and wealth – but it's a dangerous sport that demands skill, concentration, and physical and mental strength.

FACTS AND STATS

- » CAR NAME: Lotus 49
- » BUILT BY: Lotus Cars, UK
- » DESIGNED BY: Colin Chapman and Maurice Philippe
- » NUMBER BUILT: 9
- » RACED BETWEEN: 1967–1968
- » POWERED BY: 410 hp V8 Ford Cosworth DFV
- » TOP SPEED: 300 kph (approx.)
- » GEARS: 5-speed manual
- » DRIVE: Rear-wheel drive
- » DIMENSIONS: Length: 4 m; Width: 1.9 m; Height: 0.8 m; Weight: 530 kg

SAFETY LAST

The 1960s were a golden era for Formula One – but it was also the deadliest decade. The crashes and high numbers of drivers and spectators killed was simply accepted as part of the sport. Safety was hardly considered: drivers didn't wear seat belts or fireproof suits; races weren't stopped even after fatal accidents; spectators stood right next to the track; cars often caught fire after crashes, were difficult to get out of, and barriers were made from flammable straw bales.

THE LIGHTWEIGHT, LIGHTNING-FAST LOTUS

With its fat tyres, gleaming exhaust pipes and ray-gun nose, the Lotus 49 is one of the most beautiful racing cars ever made. Its 'stressed member' design, with the engine attached directly onto the chassis and rear-wheel suspension, made the car the lightest and fastest on the track – virtually every Formular One car since has followed this idea. Like all racing cars at the time, the Lotus 49 had no downforce creating wings at the front and back, meaning it was harder to control. Drivers sat right next to the fuel tanks – a situation described as "like sitting in a bathtub full of petrol".

HOW THE FORMULA ONE RACING CAR CHANGED THE WORLD

Ever since the first Grand Prix was held at Silverstone, UK, in 1950, Formula One has excited, thrilled and entertained millions of fans worldwide. It brings tourists to the host countries, has created thousands of jobs, and the technological advances made for the racing cars can be used for all sorts of other road vehicles. Formula One has also announced that it will become carbon neutral by 2030.

SLOW ROAD TO SAFETY

Throughout the 1960s, 29 Formula One drivers were killed, including Jim Clark. As the death toll mounted, some drivers tried to convince track operators to introduce safety measures such as building proper crash barriers and cutting down trackside trees, but progress was slow. Nowadays, safety in Formula One is of great importance and fatalities are rare.

COMMERCIAL JET AIRLINER
FLY THE FRIENDLY SKIES

Throughout its 50 years of service, the Boeing 747 has cruised high above the clouds carrying over three and a half billion passengers all over the world. Held aloft by four turbofan engines attached to its swept-back wings, and with the unique top deck rising above the fuselage, the 747 Jumbo Jet is one of the most successful and iconic airliners ever built.

FACTS AND STATS

» **AIRCRAFT TYPE:** Wide-body jet airliner
» **MANUFACTURED BY:** Boeing Commercial Airplanes, USA
» **FIRST 747 FLIGHT:** 1969
» **NUMBER OF 747S BUILT:** 1,558
» **CREW:** 14–18 (approx. including pilot and co-pilot)
» **PASSENGERS:** 366 (in 3 classes)
» **PICTURED MODEL POWERED BY:** 4 x Pratt and Whitney JT9D-7F turbofans
» **TOP SPEED:** 969 kph
» **CRUISING SPEED:** 895 kph
» **FUELLED BY:** Jet fuel (4.5 l used per minute)
» **MAX ALTITUDE:** 13,700 m
» **RANGE:** 9,800 km
» **DIMENSIONS:** Length: 71 m; Width: 6 m; Wingspan: 60 m; Height: 19 m

DOUBLE-DECKER

The raised section on top of the fuselage is called the 'hump' and is unique to the 747. This is where the top deck is located, reached from the lower deck by a staircase. At the front is the cockpit, and behind that is a large area used for first-class seats or a luxurious passenger lounge.

COCKPIT

Two pilots sit side by side in the cockpit, where they control the plane (with some help from the autopilot) from take-off to landing. With its hundreds of switches, dials and buttons, a 747's cockpit is extremely complicated. However, the physical rules of flight these giant aircraft must follow are exactly the same as they were way back in 1903 when the Wright brothers first took to the sky (see page 38).

LANDING GEAR

747s have a total of 18 wheels – two at the front (the 'nose-wheels'), and four sets of four underneath the wings (the 'main landing gear'). The tyres are filled with nitrogen gas because, unlike oxygen, it doesn't expand and contract when exposed to changing temperatures and air pressures; too much expansion and contraction weakens tyres and can cause them to explode.

THE FIRST AIRLINERS

As soon as they became large enough in the 1920s, propeller-driven aircraft were used to carry people and small amounts of cargo, but it wasn't until the invention of the jet engine that passenger airliners (also called 'commercial' airliners) really 'took off'. The first jet-powered airliner was the de Havilland DH.106 Comet. This stylish plane began carrying passengers in 1952, giving them a faster, quieter and smoother journey than the propeller aircraft it replaced. The Boeing 747 was the first really big passenger airliner, and made flying cheaper and safer than ever before.

STILL THE FASTEST

In the 1960s it took four engines to lift a plane the size of a 747 into the air. Modern wide-body airliners, such as the Airbus A350, only need two engines to make them fly. However, the 747 'Queen of the Sky' is still the fastest of them all, with modern variants able to hit a top speed of over 1,046 kilometres per hour – that's quick enough to travel the length of three football fields in only one second.

HOW THE COMMERCIAL AIRLINER CHANGED THE WORLD

There was a time when only wealthy people could afford the speed and convenience offered by air travel, either by rigid airship (see page 48) or propeller aircraft. The arrival of the commercial jet airliner and the introduction of the enormous Boeing 747 changed everything, allowing more people to step on board and travel, safely and swiftly, all around the world.

SATURN V

MOON ROCKET

In 1961, American president John F. Kennedy said: "I believe that this nation should commit itself to achieving the goal of landing a man on the Moon and returning him safely to Earth." Just eight years later, in 1969, his ambition was fulfilled when three brave astronauts left our planet behind on a raging column of fire created by their Saturn V rocket. After travelling together through the silence of space, Neil Armstrong and Edwin 'Buzz' Aldrin made history by setting foot on the dusty white surface of the Moon.

FACTS AND STATS

» **VEHICLE TYPE:** Super heavy-lift launch vehicle

» **OPERATED BY:** National Aeronautics and Space Administration (NASA), USA

» **APOLLO 11 LAUNCH DATE:** 16 July 1969

» **LAUNCHED FROM:** John F. Kennedy Space Center, Florida, USA

» **NUMBER OF SATURN VS LAUNCHED:** 13

» **CREW:** 3 (commander, command module pilot and lunar module pilot)

» **FUELLED BY:** Kerosene and liquid oxygen (1st stage), liquid hydrogen and liquid oxygen (2nd and 3rd stages)

» **THRUST AT LAUNCH:** 34.5 million newtons

» **TOP SPEED:** 38,624 kph

» **DIMENSIONS:** Total height: 110.6 m; Width: 10 m; Weight (fully fuelled): 2,800 tonnes; Gas volume: 2,000 m²

THE APOLLO PROGRAM

NASA's Apollo program's (1961–1972) aim was to land humans on the Moon. The first crewed mission tested the Command Service Module (CSM) in orbit around Earth, then came a journey to the Moon and 10 lunar orbits (no landing). Six missions landed on the Moon: Apollo 11, 12, 14, 15, 16 and 17; Apollo 13 had to turn back after an equipment malfunction.

THE COMMAND MODULE

This was the only part of the Saturn V that returned to Earth. The crew sat side by side, surrounded by their instruments and control panels. While the Lunar Module (and two astronauts) was on the Moon's surface, the tiny Command Module (CM) remained in orbit. After the return journey, the CM's heat shield protected the astronauts from the blistering temperatures caused by re-entering the Earth's atmosphere. Parachutes slowed the CM on its final descent into the sea.

THE LUNAR MODULE

This was the spacecraft that took its two-astronaut crew down to the Moon's surface, served as their base as they explored and took samples, and carried them back up to the orbiting CM. After docking and the transfer of crew, equipment and samples back to the CM was completed, the Lunar Module was jettisoned (detached and allowed to fall away).

TOWERS OF POWER

As the tallest, heaviest and most powerful rockets ever built, the Saturn Vs were truly awe-inspiring. Packed with enough fuel to drive a car 800 times around the Earth, and with five engines spewing fire and smoke and burning one tonne of fuel per second, they possessed the sheer brute power to pierce the sky and enter space.

STAGE 1

Saturn Vs were split into three separate Stages. Stage 1 was the biggest. Its job was to propel the rocket upward – and by the time it reached 67 kilometres high, it was travelling at an incredible 8,278 kilometres per hour. At its base were five Rocketdyne F-1 engines; the four outer engines could move to steer the rocket during flight. The fuel tanks sat over the engines, and when they ran dry Stage 1 was jettisoned.

STAGE 2

Powered by five Rocketdyne J-2 engines, Stage 2's task was to push the rocket out of the upper atmosphere and beyond Earth's gravitational pull. When that was achieved (at about 175 kilometres), it too was dumped.

STAGE 3

This was the smallest Stage. Inside was the Command Module, the Lunar Module, and the three astronauts. After a few orbits of the Earth, Stage 3's single J-2 engine fired and the long journey to the Moon – travelling at 38,624 kilometres per hour – began.

HOW THE SATURN V CHANGED THE WORLD

What NASA achieved in the short years between President Kennedy's speech and the Apollo Moon landings was extraordinary. There are now many space agencies around the world that are experimenting with multi-use rockets, making plans to revisit the Moon and even Mars. It's amazing to think a person could have watched the *Wright Flyer* (see page 38) take off in 1903, and still be alive to witness the first Saturn V roar into space 64 years later. Seeing Earth from the Moon gave humans a new perspective; as Apollo astronaut James Irwin said: "That beautiful, warm, living object looked so fragile, so delicate. Seeing that has to change a person."

TRUCK
HEAVY HAULERS

Trucks are used all over the world to haul every kind of cargo, and it's the Americans who build them biggest. This chrome-covered king of the road is the Peterbilt 379. The first of over 200,000 built drove off the assembly line decades ago, but it's still a favourite among truckers. The Peterbilt starts up – comes *alive* – with a rattle, a shake and a ground-trembling growl. Sunlight gleams on acres of chrome, exhaust stacks boom, and off this big rig rolls on 18 mighty wheels.

FACTS AND STATS

- » **MODEL:** Peterbilt 379
- » **CLASS:** Class 8 (heaviest)
- » **TRUCK TYPE:** Conventional cab
- » **BUILT BY:** Peterbilt, Texas, USA
- » **MANUFACTURED:** 1987–2007
- » **NUMBER BUILT:** 230,000
  (80 per cent still in operation)
- » **BODY DESIGN:** 2-door truck with 2-door sleeper cabin
- » **ENGINE MANUFACTURED BY:** Various including Caterpillar, Cummins and Detroit Diesel
- » **ENGINE TYPE:** Turbodiesel (various hps)
- » **TOP SPEED:** 140 kph (approx.)
- » **DIMENSIONS:** Length: 22 m; Width: 2.6 m; Height: 4 m (US truck average)

ENGINE

This type of truck, where the engine is housed in front of the driver, is called 'conventional'. The other type, where the driver sits over the engine, is called a 'cab-over-engine' (COE) or 'flat-nose'.

CARGO BY COMBUSTION ENGINE

It did not take inventors long to realise that a vehicle powered by a combustion engine could carry cargo faster and further than horses and boats. The first truck (or 'lorry') was invented in 1895 by a German mechanical engineer called Karl Benz. More designs by other inventors followed. Most had petrol engines and could haul about two tonnes. However, trucks only began to rival the horse and cart from the 1920s, when engines became more powerful and reliable, air-filled tyres replaced solid rubber, and brakes and steering improved.

SLEEPER CABIN

Long-haul drivers sometimes have to travel thousands of kilometres over several days, so they need to stop and rest every ten hours or so. Behind the driver's cab is a cosy sleeper cabin with a wide bed, lots of storage, a gas cooker, sink and heater.

HOW THE TRUCK CHANGED THE WORLD

Powerful, mass-produced trucks like the Peterbilt 379 transport billions of tonnes of cargo worldwide, from factories to ports, depots, warehouses and shops. They can haul anything, as long as they have the right kind of trailer. Trucks travel quickly, cover long distances and, unlike trains, can reach anywhere so long as there's a road; they can even cross seas on ships and ferries. Without trucks like the magnificent Peterbilts, we wouldn't be able to deliver the goods we need, on time and intact.

TAILOR-MADE TRUCK

Truck drivers spend a lot of time in their vehicles, and some like to customise them and make them feel like home. Peterbilt truckers can choose virtually any colour, pattern or design they like for the outer paintwork, as well as adding decorative lights and lots of shiny chrome for the exhaust stacks, air filters and front grills.

CHASSIS AND WHEELS

The chassis is where the trailer attaches to the truck; some trucks come with longer chassis so they can haul bigger trailers. The trailer's front weight is supported on the truck's rear wheels. Wires connect the trailer's brakes, as well as the brake and indicator lights, to the truck so the driver can control them from the cab.

CONTAINER SHIP
GIANTS OF THE SEA

The OOCL *Hong Kong* is one of the biggest cargo ships in the world – every time she comes into port she's loaded up with over 21,000 cargo containers. Stood on end, she'd be nearly 100 metres taller than the Shard in London, UK, and her deck area is as large as four football fields. Every year, ships like *Hong Kong* carry a total of nearly two billion tonnes of cargo all over the world, supplying shops with clothes, books, furniture, toys, electrical equipment and much more.

FACTS AND STATS

» **VESSEL NAME:** OOCL *Hong Kong*

» **CLASS:** G-class ultra-large container ship

» **NUMBER OF CLASS BUILT:** 6

» **OWNED BY:** Orient Overseas Container Line Ltd, Hong Kong

» **BUILT BY:** Samsung Heavy Industries, South Korea

» **LAUNCHED:** December 2016

» **CREW:** 20–30

» **ROUTE:** Asia to Europe (77-day round trip)

» **CARGO CAPACITY:** 21,413 cargo containers

» **POWERED BY:** 107,400 hp Wartsila-Sulzer RTA96-C diesel engine

» **TOP SPEED:** 39 kph

» **CRUISING SPEED:** 27 kph

» **DIMENSIONS:** Length: 400 m; Width (or 'Beam'): 59 m; Draught: 16 m

SUPERSTRUCTURE

This is where the crew live, eat and rest between work shifts. Each sailor has their own cabin, and they eat together in a refectory. At the top is the bridge, from where the ship is controlled.

TUGBOAT

Slow, heavy vessels like the *Hong Kong* cannot make the tiny speed and movement adjustments needed to dock and manoeuvre in and out of ports. To help, tugboats use their powerful engines to nudge, push and pull container ships wherever they need to go.

STEP 1. ARRIVAL AT PORT

A cargo container's journey begins when it's packed with goods (which can be anything from food to furniture) at the factory or manufacturing plant and loaded onto a freight train or truck. The train or truck then carries it to the port.

STEP 2. WAITING IN PORT

Upon arrival, the container is moved from the train or truck into a stack in the port's storage yard. Containers are transported by reach stackers, which are a bit like forklift trucks, or gantry cranes that move either on wheels or tracks. Computers keep a record of where every single container is placed.

CONTAINER

Shipping containers are designed to be transported by truck, train and ship, which means they don't need to be unpacked and reloaded at each stage of their journey. They can be stacked like building blocks, and have a unique number stamped on the outside, so they can be tracked wherever they go, including their location on the ship.

HOW THE CONTAINER SHIP CHANGED THE WORLD

Before shipping containers and container ships, goods were packed up into differently sized crates, boxes or sacks, and piled in ship holds as well as could be managed; the process was slow, inefficient and costly. Now, everything is loaded inside identical, secure cargo containers that can be tracked and stacked from a journey's start to its end. With the click of a button, people can order something from the other side of the world and it will be carried to them by container ship faster and more cheaply than ever before.

STRAIGHT SIDES

Container ships like the *Hong Kong* have straight sides to allow as many containers as possible to be stacked inside.

OOCL HONG KONG
HONG KONG

STEP 3. TO THE SHIP

When the ship has safely docked, the container is loaded onto a terminal tractor. This quickly moves it to the quayside next to the ship. Terminal tractors can be operated by a driver, or by a computer.

STEP 4. LOADING UP

Huge gantry cranes pick up the containers and place them inside or on top of the ship. Computers make sure they're stacked in the right place for maximum time efficiency: containers that need to be unloaded first are stacked near the top; containers that need to be unloaded last are placed at the bottom.

STEP 5. JOURNEY AND DELIVERY

The ship sets sail when all the containers are safely secured and drops them off at their designated ports. The unloading process is the exact same as loading but carried out in reverse.

SPACE SHUTTLE
THE REUSABLE SPACE-PLANE

Made up of two and a half million moving parts, the Space Shuttle was one of the most complicated and expensive vehicles ever created. Unlike the Saturn V rocket that could only be used once, the Space Shuttle was designed to blast itself and its crew into orbit, carry out its mission, and return to Earth to be used again. Five Shuttles were built – *Columbia, Challenger, Discovery, Atlantis* and *Endeavour* – and together they flew 133 successful missions over 30 years. However, two Shuttles were destroyed and their crews killed in tragic accidents – a reminder of the dangers of space travel and the bravery of the astronauts who dare to face it.

FACTS AND STATS

- » **SHUTTLE NAME:** *Discovery*
- » **OPERATED BY:** National Aeronautics and Space Administration (NASA), USA
- » **BASED AT:** Kennedy Space Center, Florida, USA
- » **ORBITER BUILT BY:** Boeing and Rockwell, USA
- » **EXTERNAL TANK BUILT BY:** Lockheed Martin and Martin Marietta, USA
- » **SOLID ROCKET BOOSTERS BUILT BY:** United Space Alliance, Thiokol and Alliant Techsystems, USA
- » **NUMBER OF CLASS BUILT:** 5 (plus non-orbital test Shuttle *Enterprise*)
- » **FIRST LAUNCH IN SHUTTLE PROGRAM:** *Columbia*, 12 April 1981
- » **FINAL LAUNCH IN SHUTTLE PROGRAM:** *Atlantis*, 8 July 2011
- » **CREW:** 6–8
- » **FUELLED BY:** 721,897 litres of liquid hydrogen and liquid oxygen (in external tank); 907,185 kg of ammonium perchlorate composite propellant (APCP) (in solid rocket boosters)
- » **SPEED IN ORBIT:** 28,000 kph
- » **ORBIT HEIGHT:** 186–644 km
- » **DISTANCE TRAVELLED BY ALL SHUTTLES:** 872,906,390 km
- » **TIME IN SPACE BY ALL SHUTTLES:** 1,334 days, 1 hour, 36 minutes and 44 seconds
- » **ORBITER DIMENSIONS:** Length: 37 m; Wingspan: 23.8 m; Height: 17.9 m

CREW COMPARTMENT

This was the only pressurized part of the OV. At the top was the flight deck, and beneath was where the crew slept, ate, washed and went to the toilet. The bottom deck contained equipment and the toilet. Access for EVA ('extra-vehicular activity', or 'spacewalking') was through an airlock – a small, airtight room allowing astronauts to safely move to and from outer space.

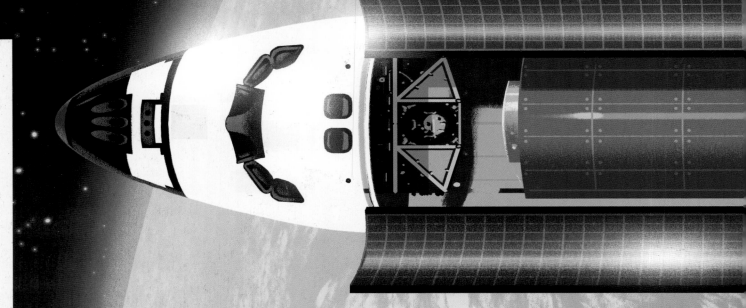

LAUNCHED LIKE A ROCKET

The Space Shuttle was made up of several parts: the Orbitar Vehicle (the OV, pictured), an External Tank (ET) and two Solid Rocket Boosters (SRBs). Before launch, the OV and SRBs were attached to the ET, then transported to the launch pad. When the crew was on board and all safety checks complete, the OV's three RS-25 engines (fuelled by the ET) ignited, followed by the SRBs. Up roared the Shuttle, trailing fire and smoke; after 123 seconds the SRBs detached and floated into the sea on parachutes to be used again. Then the empty ET was jettisoned and the Orbiter carried out the final push to enter low Earth Orbit (under 1,000 kilometres high).

ORBITED LIKE A SATELLITE

Once in space, the OV could carry out lots of tasks, including deploying satellites and telescopes into orbit and exploratory probes into space; helping to construct the International Space Station; and using a specially built laboratory called Spacelab for experiments. The longest mission was undertaken by *Columbia* in 1996 and lasted 17 days and 15 hours.

REMOTE MANIPULATOR SYSTEM

Controlled from the flight deck, a robotic arm – nicknamed 'Canadarm' because it was built by a Canadian company – was used to move payloads and astronauts around or out of the cargo bay.

LANDED LIKE A GLIDER

After leaving orbit, the OV was designed to be flown in the same way as an aeroplane: it had an aerodynamic shape, two wings and a rudder (the 'vertical stabiliser') to control pitch, roll and yaw, and retractable landing gear. Re-entry into the atmosphere began at 120 kilometres high and 25 times the speed of sound (8,575 metres per second). As it glided all the way from space to the runway, the OV used its descent angle, speed brake and finally a parachute and wheel brakes to slow it down to a stop.

THERMAL PROTECTION SYSTEM

The Shuttle was covered in a layer of tiles to protect it and the crew from the blistering heat created by re-entry into the atmosphere. The strongest layer was put on the underside and nose (the black parts) because they reached temperatures of up to 1,600°C.

HOW THE SPACE SHUTTLE CHANGED THE WORLD

During its long career, the Space Shuttle deployed and repaired invaluable astronomical equipment, such as the Hubble Space Telescope, launched space probes to explore the Solar System, as well as satellites to study Earth, and helped build and maintain the International Space Station. As the first reusable spacecraft in history, it increased our knowledge of our world as well as space, and paved the way for more advanced future orbital vehicles.

SMART CAR
GREEN MOTORVATION

Since their invention over 100 years ago, the automobile (see page 36) has given people the freedom to travel far without having to rely on public transport. However, the billions of fossil-fuel-burning cars that drive on the roads today are having a devastating impact on the environment. On average, one car produces over four and a half tonnes of harmful carbon dioxide gas into the atmosphere every year – a major cause of global warming, allergies and disease. Because of this, many manufacturers are designing cars that are kinder to the environment – like the smart little Smart car.

SMALL IN THE CITY

Many cities and towns were built centuries ago and, with their narrow roads and tight corners, were not designed with large, noisy, pollution-emitting cars in mind. Cars fill the air with fumes and noise, and clog up the streets when parked or being driven. Smart cars were designed to reduce these problems: they are only as long as most cars are wide, which means they can park with their front facing the pavement and not take up as much room; they can zip along narrow streets with ease, and because they are lightweight and have fuel-efficient engines, they don't produce as much pollution.

FACTS AND STATS

- » **CAR NAME:** Smart Fortwo
- » **TYPE OF CAR:** Subcompact
- » **MANUFACTURED BY:** Daimler AG, Germany
- » **MANUFACTURED:** 1998–present day
- » **NUMBER BUILT:** 2 million+
- » **PASSENGERS:** 2 (including driver)
- » **POWERED BY:** 89 hp 3-cylinder turbocharged engine
- » **TOP SPEED:** 145 kph
- » **AMOUNT OF FUEL USED:** 290 kilometres per litre
- » **DIMENSIONS:** Length: 2.7 m; Width: 1.7 m; Height: 1.6 m

COMPACT BUT COMFORTABLE

Although Smart cars are much smaller than ordinary cars, they have been carefully designed to be as comfortable and spacious for the driver and passenger as possible. The roof is high enough for people to sit upright, and the passenger seat is set a bit further back than the driver's to give them the maximum amount of legroom.

HOW THE SMART CAR CHANGED THE WORLD

Smart and electric cars are in the process of changing our world for the better, and will hopefully continue to do so. There is a growing desire – and desperate need – to change the way we fuel our cars, and these eco-friendly vehicles are an effective way to reduce our reliance on damaging fossil fuels such as petrol and diesel. Some countries have pledged to stop producing fossil-fuel-burning cars in favour of electric vehicles like the Smart EQ. Decisive action like this is essential if we are to save our precious planet.

ELECTRIC CARS

Many manufacturers are building cars powered by electric motors, such as the Smart EQ, the Renault Zoe, Tesla Model S, Audi e-tron, Jaguar I-Pace and Porsche Taycan. The motors run using power stored in batteries, which can be charged at public power outlets or overnight from the owner's home. Electric cars do not produce any harmful emissions, are much quieter than petrol- or diesel-powered vehicles, and can drive for several hundred kilometres before needing to recharge.

SELF-DRIVING CARS

There is another type of 'smart' vehicle – a computer-operated car that doesn't need a human driver. Self-driving cars look similar to normal ones, but they are equipped with sensors that tell them what is going on around them (such as nearby vehicles), can spot obstacles in the road and can even read road signs. Although self-driving cars are still highly experimental, and there are concerns about how safe they are compared to human-operated vehicles, it seems likely that as technology advances they will be used more and more in the future.

SHANGHAI MAGLEV
THE MAGNETIC MARVEL

On a raised track supported by thousands of concrete pillars glides a wonder of modern transport technology. The Shanghai Maglev runs for 30 kilometres between two stations in China. In that short distance, it accelerates to record-breaking speeds – and yet the ride experienced by the passengers is smoother and quieter than almost any other powered land vehicle.

FAST AND FRICTIONLESS

As the Maglev reaches its top speed, the world rushes past the windows in a blur of motion: buildings, bridges and rivers are ahead, level, and then suddenly out of sight. And yet, when passengers sit back in the comfortable seats and watch the digital speed display on the wall creep up, they hardly feel any movement at all. The Maglev does not rattle, vibrate or shake – it provides a miraculously smooth journey even as it travels faster than any other train in the world.

DRIVERLESS

The Maglev is not controlled by a driver sitting in the front cab – the only people on board as it zooms along are the passengers. That means there are no speed signals or signs along the line either. The line and trains are operated remotely from a control centre using an Automatic Train Operation (ATO) system. In case of emergency, an Automatic Train Protection (ATP) system turns on the emergency brake and brings the Maglev to a stop.

FACTS AND STATS

» **ALTERNATIVE NAME:** Shanghai Transrapid
» **MANUFACTURED BY:** Siemens and ThyssenKrupp, Germany
» **OPERATED BY:** Shanghai Maglev Transportation Development, China
» **LINE OPENED TO PUBLIC:** 2004
» **LINE LENGTH:** 30.5 km
» **STATIONS:** 2 (Shanghai Pudong International Airport and Longyang Road Station)
» **CREW:** 0
» **PASSENGERS:** 574
» **TOP SPEED:** 431 kph
» **JOURNEY TIME:** 8 minutes
» **DIMENSIONS:** Length: 153 m; Width: 3.7 m; Height: 4.2 m

FLOATING TRAIN

The Shanghai Maglev is a land vehicle, but it doesn't actually touch the ground. The Electromagnetic Suspension (EMS) system raises the whole train one and a half centimetres above the rail, allowing it to glide effortlessly through the air. This means that unlike normal trains, where wheels roll directly over steel rails, there is absolutely no friction to slow the Maglev down or cause rattling and vibrations.

MOVING BY MAGNETS

The Maglev is lifted from the ground, guided around corners and pushed forward by a series of electromagnets positioned on the train and track (called the 'guideway'). Electromagnets create magnetic fields that can repel or attract each other, and it's these that cause the train to float, speed up and slow down. Guide magnets on the side of the train keep it centred on the guideway and move it forward.

HIGH-UP HIGH SPEED

The land between Shanghai and the airport is covered with houses, high-rise apartments, shops, factories, highways, railways and waterways. The Maglev guideway had to be built high up so the trains can travel uninterrupted over all these obstacles. The guideway is built from steel and extra-strong concrete, and supported on thousands of concrete pillars.

HOW THE SHANGHAI MAGLEV CHANGED THE WORLD

Although the Shanghai Maglev only cruises at its record-breaking top speed for a few minutes each journey, it is still an extraordinary vehicle. Since the line first opened in 2004, it has shown the world how fast, safe and effective vehicles powered by electromagnetic suspension systems can be. In Japan, the experimental L0 Series Maglev train set a land speed record of 603 kilometres per hour for rail vehicles, proving that the future of Maglev travel is hurtling towards us at lightning speed.

ELECTRIC BIKE
PEDAL-ASSISTED POWER

The humble pedal bike (see Early Bicycle, page 30) has given millions of ordinary people the freedom to explore, go to work and have fun in the wider world without the need for horses or motor vehicles. And yet the bike's range is limited to how fit and strong the rider is, and how far they can pedal. However, by helping to drive the wheels, the electric bike allows any rider to travel further and faster, and even makes cycling up hills less of a strain on hard-working legs.

A LONG JOURNEY

Inventors began coming up with designs for pedal bikes powered by electric motors in the late 1890s. However, back then, electric motors and the batteries that fuelled them were not powerful enough to be truly effective. It wasn't until the 1990s that the technology was sufficiently advanced to make electric bikes worth buying. Electric bike batteries and motors are getting smaller, lighter and more powerful, meaning they can carry people further and faster with every passing year.

FACTS AND STATS

» **BIKE NAME:** FuroSystems Aventa
» **BUILT BY:** Aventa, UK
» **POWERED BY:** BAFANG rear hub electric motor
» **BATTERY:** Lithium-Ion
» **BATTERY RANGE:** 80 km
» **TOP SPEED:** 25 kph
» **DIMENSIONS:** Height: 78 cm;
  Wheelbase length: 1.1 m; Weight: 16.5 kg

E-BIKE TYPES

There are two types of electric bike. With pedal-assist bikes, or 'pedelecs' (pedal electric cycle), the motor only starts up when the rider turns the pedals, making them easier to rotate. Pedelecs are perfect for climbing hills or making cycling easier for people with weak legs or heart problems. The motor on a power-on-demand bike is operated by a throttle on the handlebar. This means the rider doesn't need to pedal at all if they don't want to, or they can switch off the motor and rely entirely on their legs to turn the pedals.

HOW THE ELECTRIC BIKE CHANGED THE WORLD

Now that rechargeable batteries and electric motors are so small, light and powerful, electric bikes are getting ever more popular all over the world. They make long journeys and hills easier to tackle, giving people of all ages and fitness levels the amazing opportunity to get out on the open road and explore, as well as improving their health. And, unlike cars and motorbikes, they don't produce the harmful emissions that cause so much environmental damage.

ENVIRONMENTALLY FRIENDLY

We now know that the fossil fuels used to power cars, lorries and motorbikes have a terrible effect on the environment. The pollution they create is heating up our planet, and damaging to our health when we breathe it in. Electric bikes do not produce any harmful emissions at all, and they have rechargeable batteries that can be used many times over. And when the electricity used to recharge them is generated using green technology such as solar or wind power, this reduces their carbon footprint even more.

PEDALLING INTO POPULARITY

For the last 30 years, electric bikes have become more and more popular all over the world, with some countries providing charging stations on the streets for cyclists to use. In 2007, 200,000 electric bikes were sold in Europe; in 2009 that number rose to 500,000; and in 2019 the number rose again to a staggering three million. China loves electric bikes even more: 16 million were sold in 2020 alone, and there are approximately 270 million in use on the roads at this time.

MARS ROVER
INTREPID PLANETARY EXPLORERS

After a journey of tens of millions of kilometres through space, this clever machine landed on Mars on 6 August 2012 and began its mission of discovery. As its name suggests, its job is to 'rove', or travel, across Mars – but it does far more than that. The Mars rover *Curiosity* collects samples, carries out experiments, gathers information about its surroundings, takes photographs and videos, and survives completely alone in the harsh Martian environment.

COMPUTER POWER

Curiosity has two identical computers – one is a back-up in case the other fails. The computer monitors and controls *Curiosity*'s many systems, tracks its exact location, and acts on NASA's transmitted instructions.

HOW THE ROVER ROVES

Curiosity uses six 50-centimetre-wide aluminium wheels on six legs to travel across the rocky, uneven surface of Mars. Each wheel is powered by its own motor. The four wheels at the front and back also have their own steering motors, allowing the rover to turn in a curve or on the spot. *Curiosity*'s body sits on a 'rocker bogie' suspension system, which keeps it level when moving over rocks, slopes and inclines. Automatic sensors stop the rover from travelling on land that would cause it to tip over.

HOW CURIOSITY COMMUNICATES

Curiosity needs to send all the information it learns about Mars back to Earth, as well as receive orders from NASA. To do this, the rover uses three radio antennae located on its back. *Curiosity* usually sends information up to one of the satellites orbiting Mars, which then beams it to Earth. Signals take an average of 14 minutes to travel between Mars and Earth.

TEMPERATURE CONTROL

A layer of insulation, electric heaters and fluid pumped through pipes keep the rover at a steady temperature – even when Mars gets as cold as -127°C.

FACTS AND STATS

» **ROVER NAME:** *Curiosity*
» **MISSION NAME:** Mars Science Laboratory (MSL)
» **MISSION DESIGNERS:** National Aeronautics and Space Administration (NASA), USA
» **MANUFACTURERED BY:** JPL, Boeing and Lockheed Martin
» **LAUNCH DATE:** 26 November 2011
» **LANDING DATE:** 6 August 2012
» **LANDING SITE:** Gale Crater, Mars
» **POWERED BY:** Radioisotope Thermoelectric Generator
» **TOP SPEED:** 4 cm per second
» **DIMENSIONS:** Length: 2.9 m; Width: 2.7 m; Height: 2.2 m

ENERGY SOURCE

Curiosity has to create all of its own power. It does this by using a Radioisotope Thermoelectric Generator, a device that converts the heat generated by radioactive substances found on Mars into electricity. This method will provide *Curiosity* with a constant source of power for at least one Martian year – or 687 Earth days.

LASER, DRILL AND DUSTER

To take rock samples, *Curiosity* can use a drill, or fire an infra-red laser. The robotic arm picks up the samples and transfers them inside the rover to be examined and analysed. The arm also has a rotating bristle brush to remove dust from the planet surface, revealing what is hidden underneath.

ROBOTIC ARM

Curiosity's flexible, movable arm has three joints (like a shoulder, elbow and wrist) and several tools at the end, which allow it to gather and examine rock and soil samples.

WAS THERE LIFE ON MARS?

By examining rocks and the atmosphere, *Curiosity* has discovered that Mars used to have a warmer climate and was home to running water and hot-water springs. This means it's possible Mars might once have supported simple lifeforms called microbes.

HOW THE MARS ROVER CHANGED THE WORLD

At the moment, Mars is too far away for astronauts to reach, so we rely on the Mars rovers to explore and gather vital information and remove some of the mystery. The more we learn from the rovers' adventures, the closer we are to a first manned mission to Mars. So, it's not just that the Mars rovers are changing our world, they might also help us find a way to live on a new one. In February 2021, a new rover, *Perseverance*, landed on Mars with the task of searching for signs of microbial life that existed in the past, as well as recording sounds from the planet's surface.

SOLAR-POWERED AEROPLANE
FLYING WITHOUT FUEL

Seen from a distance the *Solar Impulse 2* might look a bit old-fashioned: its wings are
incredibly long and fixed to the top of the fuselage, it has four propellers, and it travels slowly.
Yet this remarkable vehicle is actually very modern and uses cutting-edge technology for
a very specific task: to spread a message to everyone in the world – including you.

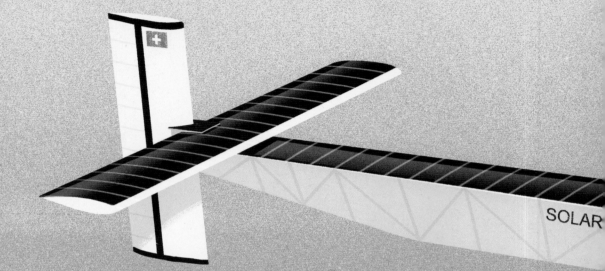

FACTS AND STATS

- » AEROPLANE NAME: *Solar Impulse 2*
- » CREW: 2 (pilot and reconnaissance systems officer (RSO))
- » FUELLED BY: Solar power
- » PROPELLED BY: 4 x 17.4 hp energy-efficient electric motors
- » TOP SPEED: 216 kph
- » AVERAGE CRUISING SPEED: 70 kph
- » RANGE: Theoretically unlimited
- » LONGEST NON-STOP FLIGHT: 117 hours, 52 minutes
- » MAX ALTITUDE: 8,534 m
- » DIMENSIONS: Length: 22.4 m; Wingspan: 72 m; Height: 6.37 m; Weight: 2.3 tonnes

NO FUEL, NO POLLUTION

The *Solar Impulse 2* is a proper aeroplane: it takes off, flies
long distances and lands under its own power, and yet it
carries absolutely no fuel. All the energy it needs to turn
the propellers and run the electrical systems is provided by
the Sun. The aeroplane's entire upper surface (an area big
enough for 1,000 people to stand) is covered in 17,248 solar
cells. The *Solar Impulse 2*'s complete reliance on renewable
energy means it creates absolutely no pollution whatsoever.

SWISS SOLAR PIONEERS

The plane was created by two Swiss men with a message. Bertrand Piccard is a doctor, pilot and explorer who was the first person to fly non-stop around the world in a balloon. (His father was Jacques Piccard who piloted the *Trieste* – see page 68). André Borschberg is an engineer and pilot with a passion for aircraft and protecting the environment.

RECORD BREAKER

The *Solar Impulse 2* was built to travel all the way around the world without using a single drop of fuel. This journey was split into stages, with André and Bertrand taking it in turns to fly. They began in the United Arab Emirates (UAE), then travelled across the Middle East, India, Myanmar, China, Japan, Hawaii, the USA, Spain, Egypt and finished up back in the UAE. The longest stage was from Japan to Hawaii and took 117 hours and 52 minutes – the longest solo flight (by time) ever made. This amazing around-the-world trip took 23.25 days of flight time and covered a distance of 42,438 kilometres.

LIGHT AS A CAR

Solar-powered aeroplanes are designed to be as lightweight as possible. In fact, the *Solar Impulse 2*'s engines have about the same horsepower rating as the *Wright Flyer* (see page 38). *Solar Impulse 2*'s wingspan is longer than a Boeing 747's (see page 86), and yet, incredibly, the whole aircraft weighs only 2,300 kilograms – about the same as a family car. This is achieved by using revolutionary lightweight materials such as carbon fibre that is three times lighter than paper, and solar panels that are only as thick as a hair.

HOW THE *SOLAR IMPULSE 2* CHANGED THE WORLD

The *Solar Impulse 2* is unlike every other vehicle in this book because it carries not passengers or cargo, but a message. By flying around the world using nothing but the power of the Sun, it shows the boundless potential offered by clean, renewable energy that doesn't use up our Earth's precious resources or create pollution. As Bertrand Piccard says: "If an aeroplane can fly day and night without fuel, the world can be much cleaner."

JOURNEY'S END

The 50 Vehicles That Changed the World have driven, flown and sailed us over huge distances, at great speeds and into dangerous places. We've looked down on the Great Pyramids from the *Solar Impulse 2*, driven through rainy Piccadilly Circus on an omnibus, raced into battle on a trireme, explored the deepest part of our oceans in the *Trieste*, and from the shuttle even seen our precious Earth hang in space like a shiny blue marble.

All these experiences have shown us that without vehicles the world we'd live in would be very small indeed. Most of us would not stray far from where we were born, and would be surrounded by unexplored lands, uncharted seas and an empty sky.

And yet, despite the incalculable progress that vehicles have given us, we also know our dependence on them is causing great harm to our planet. The fossil fuels burned by so many internal-combustion-powered vehicles creates vast quantities of greenhouse gases. These gases are heating our atmosphere and changing our climate, the effects of which are already causing (among other things) rising sea levels and extreme weather conditions, such as drought, floods and forest fires.

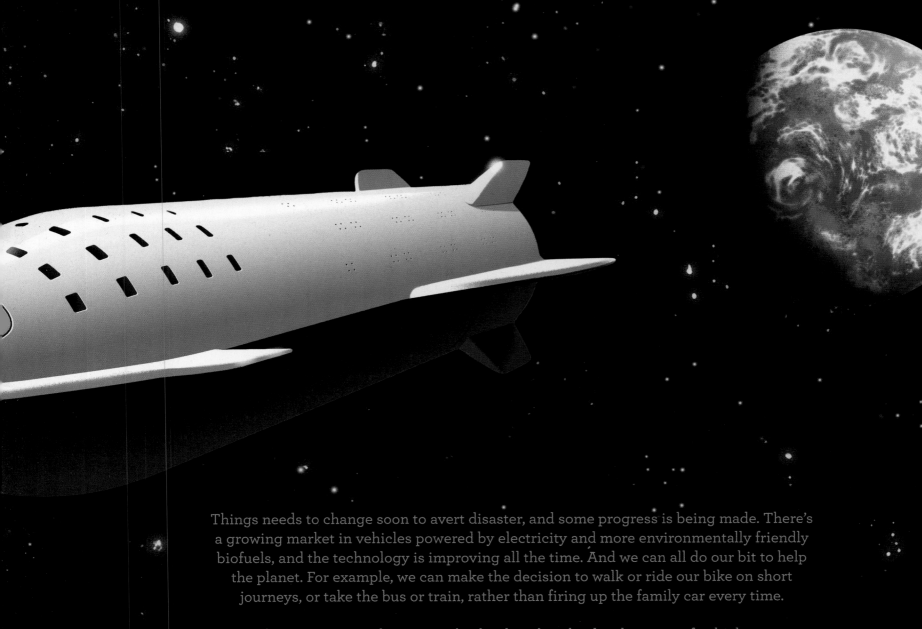

Things needs to change soon to avert disaster, and some progress is being made. There's a growing market in vehicles powered by electricity and more environmentally friendly biofuels, and the technology is improving all the time. And we can all do our bit to help the planet. For example, we can make the decision to walk or ride our bike on short journeys, or take the bus or train, rather than firing up the family car every time.

One thing we've seen for sure in this book is that the development of vehicles never stops. Scientists and engineers are constantly experimenting and working to improve on what has gone before: driverless cars, faster trains, bigger container ships. And where will the increasing interest in space travel take us? Plans are already afoot for more crewed trips to the Moon, there is serious research being undertaken by the national space agencies and private companies to build a permanent base on Mars for people to live in, and many more journeys by uncrewed probes are scheduled to further explore the rest of our planetary neighbours and their moons.

The future of vehicles is exciting. Perhaps, in a few decades time, there will be 50 new types of vehicle that will change the world all over again, just as Stephenson's steam locomotive and the Wright brothers' *Flyer* did. Perhaps you will drive one yourself.

PERHAPS YOU'LL EVEN *INVENT* ONE!

GLOSSARY

AERODYNAMIC Having a smooth shape that helps vehicles move faster through the air.

ALTITUDE The height of an object above the Earth's ground or sea level.

AUTOPILOT/AUTOMATIC PILOT A device that controls an aircraft, ship or spacecraft without the need of a human.

AVIATOR A pilot.

AXLE A rod that connects wheels, allowing them to turn at the same time.

BALLAST TANK A water tank on a submarine: filling it with water causes the submarine to dive; pumping it with air causes the submarine to surface.

BOW The front of a ship, boat or submarine.

BUOYANCY The ability or tendency of a vessel to float in water.

CAPSIZE When a ship or boat tips over.

CARBON NEUTRAL When the activities of a city, country or company does not produce an excess of carbon dioxide.

CARGO Goods and products transported by aeroplanes or ships.

CHASSIS The base structure of a vehicle, onto which the wheels, engine, seats, etc. are attached.

COMBUSTION ENGINE An engine that creates energy by burning ('combusting') fuel with an oxidizer (usually air).

CONTRAPTION A machine or device.

EXHAUST PIPE The vent in an engine through which gas waste is released.

FLEET A group of ships.

FOSSIL FUEL Fuels found underground that cannot be replaced after they are used (non-renewable), such as coal and oil.

FREIGHT Goods and products transported by rail or truck.

FRIGATE A light warship.

FUNNEL A chimney on a ship or steam engine for venting gaseous waste from the engine.

FUSELAGE The body of an aeroplane.

HULL The main watertight body of a ship, including the bottom, sides and deck.

HYDRAULIC A technology that uses liquids (often water) and pressure to create energy.

KEEL The long timber or metal structure at the bottom of a ship onto which the frame is attached.

LOCOMOTIVE A powered vehicle that runs on rails and hauls passenger and freight trains.

MANUFACTURER A company or organization that makes something.

MASS-PRODUCED The large-scale and often automated production of identical (or 'standardised') objects.

MAST A pole on a ship onto which the sails and rigging are attached.

MERCHANT A trader or salesperson.

MOSAIC An image or pattern created using small coloured tiles, pieces of stone or glass.

NAVAL Relating to ships (usually military) owned and operated by a country.

NUCLEAR REACTOR A type of power generator used in power stations and large naval vessels.

ONAGERS A species of wild ass (which is similar to a donkey) originating from Asia; 'onager' means 'wild ass'.

PIONEERING The creation of new ideas and methods of doing something.

PISTON Part of an engine that uses gas or liquid to push a cylinder up and down inside a tube, to make a vehicle move.

PREHISTORIC The period of history before the invention of written records.

PROPELLER A spinning device that pushes a ship or submarine through the water, or powers an aeroplane through the air.

PROW The front of a ship, boat or submarine.

RENEWABLE ENERGY Energy generated using sources that can be replaced, such as wind, hydraulic or solar power.

REVOLUTION A dramatic change from the way things were to something new.

RUDDER A flat, movable device used to steer a ship, boat or submarine.

SHAFT HORSE POWER (SHP) A unit measurement of power.

SPOKES/SPOKED Rods connecting a wheel hub to the wheel rim; spoked wheels are strong as well as lightweight.

STERN The back/rear of a ship, boat or submarine.

STREAMLINED A shape that allows vehicles to move through air and water more quickly.

STRUTS Metal or wooden parts that give shape and strength to a structure.

SUSPENSION The springs and/or shock absorbers that support a vehicle on its wheels and make travel smoother.

THROTTLE A device that controls how much fuel or power is given to an engine.

THRUST The propulsive force created by a rocket or jet engine, which moves the vehicle forward and/or up.

TRACTION ENGINE A steam locomotive used on roads (not rails).

TURBINE A device that uses the flow of fluid to generate energy.

VESSEL A large ship.

WARPED When something gets bent or twisted out of shape, often because of damp or heat.

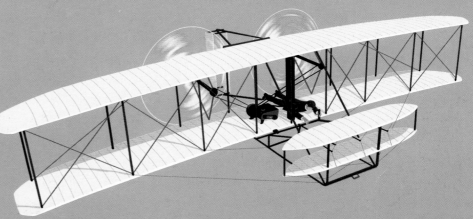

INDEX